kiddiwalks
Cambridge

Charlotte Moerman

COUNTRYSIDE BOOKS
NEWBURY BERKSHIRE

COUNTRYSIDE BOOKS
3 Catherine Road
Newbury, Berkshire

To view our complete range of books,
please visit us at
www.countrysidebooks.co.uk

ISBN 978 1 84674 277 4

With grateful thanks to my parents,
Lynne and Ray Caley,
for their invaluable help and support.

Designed by Peter Davies, Nautilus Design
Produced through MRM Associates Ltd., Reading
Typeset by CJWT Solutions, St Helens
Printed by Information Press, Oxford

Contents

Area Map Showing the Locations of the Walks

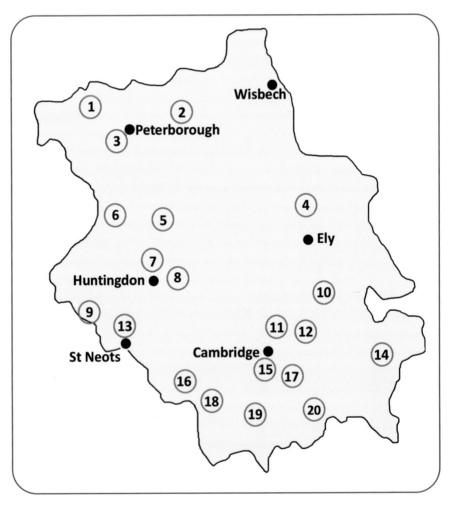

Contents

PUBLISHER'S NOTE

We hope that you obtain considerable enjoyment from this book; great care has been taken in its preparation. Although at the time of publication all routes followed public rights of way or permitted paths, diversion orders can be made and permissions withdrawn.

We cannot, of course, be held responsible for such diversion orders and any inaccuracies in the text which result from these or any other changes to the routes, nor any damage which might result from walkers trespassing on private property. We are anxious though that all details covering the walks are kept up to date and would therefore welcome information from readers which would be relevant to future editions.

The simple sketch maps that accompany the walks in this book are based on notes made by the author whilst checking out the routes on the ground. They are designed to show you how to reach the start, to point out the main features of the overall circuit and they contain a progression of numbers that relate to the paragraphs of the text.

However, for the benefit of a proper map, we do recommend that you purchase the relevant Ordnance Survey sheet covering your walk. The Ordnance Survey maps are widely available, especially through booksellers and local newsagents.

Introduction

Since moving from the Big City to Cambridgeshire, I've thrown myself into country living. I have trodden more farm tracks, river banks and woodland paths than you can shake a stick at, as have my accommodating husband and three sons. Though at first we had to convince the boys that it was okay – wellies were meant to get muddy – they now like to think of themselves as seasoned ramblers. Especially when it's blackberry season, they have a container apiece and a determined glint in their eyes!

These days we are not such novices in the country and, as I am forever impressing upon the children that it's nice to share, we would like to recommend these interesting Cambridgeshire places in which to flex your walking muscles.

The most successful walks are not force-fed but fun (and free!) so I have tried to keep the tone of these walks as light-hearted as possible, with ideas for things to look at, chat about, or do along the way. The possibilities are endless. If in doubt, why not propose a scavenger hunt? To help with activities, take a container, some string and a pen knife in your backpack – also useful for cutting down villainous nettles when the need arises – along with a good stick which you can find together en route.

The walks are generally 2–4 miles long, so most are best suited to robust children rather than toddlers. That said, the country park circuits are all buggy-suitable and can be shortened for tired little legs – which always seem to get an extra boost of energy when a playground is in sight! The times needed for the walks are approximate and may be increased by an absorbing game, activity or a hearty lunch.

With 20 circuits to explore, I have aimed for variety. There are walks through some of the county's ancient woodland, in and around pretty villages and along historic leafy tracks such as the Icknield Way, apparently the oldest road in Britain. There are routes along majestic rivers, around glittering lakes and beside humble but VIP fenland drains.

Nature reserves, airfields and former gravel works are all taken in at some point. And last but not least, although this is East Anglia, I have managed to pull a few hills out of the bag, though rest assured there'll be no mountaineering here, thank you very much!

Included are recommendations for places to feed and water the hungry walkers. It's not a bad idea to keep a snack and a drink in the backpack too. Don't forget sun cream, sunhats and a pair of long socks apiece for unexpected nettles in summer. It is assumed that children able to walk these distances are old enough to be sensible but do be careful near unfenced water, footpath-less roads and farmers' electric fences.

Directions are given for those arriving at the starting point of each walk by car but many of the walks can be accessed using public transport. Visit www.cambridgeshire.gov.uk/transport/around/buses for details.

I would like to extend grateful thanks to the many friends who have helped test drive these routes and photographed their off-spring along the way. Also to the rangers and local residents who helped with advice about their patch, and to the kindly families who I didn't know but asked to photograph their children regardless! Finally, my biggest thank you to my husband, sons and trusty parents for pacing out the walks, reading the draft texts and sampling the country pubs. It was a tough job but somebody had to do it!

Charlotte Moerman

Barnack

Who Needs a Theme Park?

The first stile of the walk

Get ready to zoom up and down hills, arms aloft and squealing, because on this walk you'll visit nature's own rollercoaster. Once a medieval quarry, the Barnack Hills and Holes Nature Reserve is now a dash-up-and-down heaven, complete with day-glo lights (well, glow-worms anyway). There's also a house that sounds like a footballer's home, a windmill with an unusual hat, and a pub with the best bangers and mash in town. So what are you waiting for?

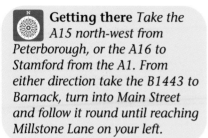

Getting there *Take the A15 north-west from Peterborough, or the A16 to Stamford from the A1. From either direction take the B1443 to Barnack, turn into Main Street and follow it round until reaching Millstone Lane on your left.*

Length of walk 3½ miles.
Time to allow 2 hours.
Terrain A lovely varied walk, but beware the short stretch of country road. The nature reserve is very uneven so is not suitable for buggies.
Start/Parking The lane outside the Millstone pub. (GR: TF 077049).
Map OS Explorer 234
Refreshments The Millstone is a classic country pub with real ales, a courtyard garden and a warm welcome. Portion sizes are generous – don't miss the Lincolnshire sausages – and there's a good choice on the children's menu. Tel. 01780 740296.

1 From the pub, turn left down Millstone Lane. Turn right at the end, admiring the 13th-century stone arch further along. This was once part of the parish church but is now set into a garden wall. At the tree roundabout, turn right and follow the road as it bends left, past an old pub whose name – the Fox – is revealed by the door-knocker. At the church, carefully cross over and take an alleyway to the right of the post office. At the end of this long passage, follow a footpath right, keeping the cricket ground wall on your right. Continue straight

Fun Things to See and Do ◆

Though they say the lights in the nature reserve on warm summer nights are glow-worms, what if they were really aliens? Why don't *you* **turn Martian for a day**? Imagine you've just landed; climb out of your spaceship and look around. Use your Martian walkie-talkie to provide a running commentary to Mother Ship about what you see on your walk. Don't forget to use your best Martian voice!

1

on at the next junction of footpaths, past the bowling green on your right. Go through a wooden kissing gate and emerge into a meadow. Off to the right is the Grade I listed Walcot Hall. Who thinks it might belong to a famous footballer?

2 Proceed alongside the hedge which eventually dips off left, then continue straight towards the house on the far side. After the black kissing gate, cross the road and walk left of the house – what is the year on the date stone? Now head across the arable field towards houses, then over a stile and into a triangular meadow. Make towards the buildings and cross the stile left of the barns. Turn right onto the footpath through the village of Southorpe, looking out for the pair of Barnack Rag blocks by the telephone box. Walk on past thinning houses, as if leaving the village. Unfortunately, the footpath peters out, so do watch out for traffic. Who first spots 'Two Hoots'?

3 After passing Stud Farm, but before reaching Grange Farm, turn right through a wooden gate to follow the bridleway sign. Follow the track through a gateway, then veer diagonally

Heading onto the Ermine Way

right and up through a yellow-tipped wooden gate at the crest. Now walk for a considerable way in a rod-straight line along what is part of the old Roman road, Ermine Street. After drystone walls, farm tracks and assorted fields, you'll eventually meet the corner of the formal perimeter walls to Walcot Hall. Continue straight on, keeping the wall on your right. Stop and peek in at the magnificent lime avenue, and then continue until the wall comes to an end. Pass through a double set of gates to join the

he Walk

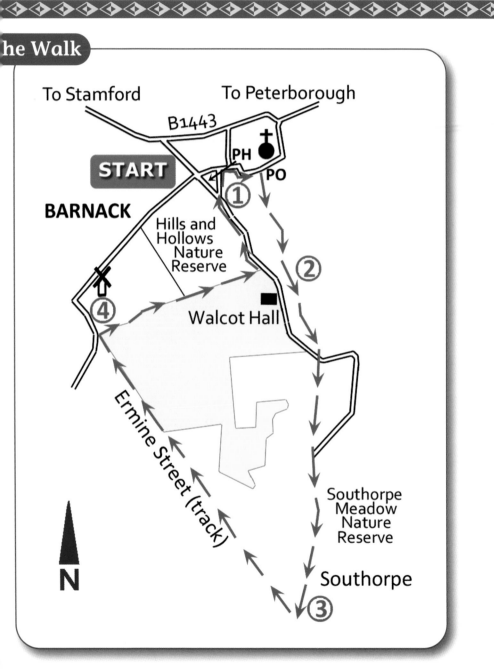

To Stamford

To Peterborough

B1443

PH

PO

START

BARNACK

①

Hills and Hollows Nature Reserve

②

Walcot Hall

④

Ermine Street (track)

Southorpe Meadow Nature Reserve

Southorpe

③

N

road on a bend. Now turn sharp right following the corner of the perimeter wall.

4 With the wall still on your right, glance left across the fields to the 18th-century Barnack windmill with its distinctive white ogee cap. Proceed until reaching the gate into the Hills and Holes Nature Reserve. Continue alongside the wall, through another gate, until you reach the reserve corner. Don't go through the exit, but turn left to continue along the irresistibly fun and twisty path. Ignore two options to rejoin the road, but go through a further gate before finally taking a kissing gate to the right onto a lay-by. Carefully cross the road and head back on the footpath, taking the right fork to the pub.

◆ Background Notes ◆

The impressive **Hills and Holes** were formed when the area was quarried for limestone known as Barnack Rag. The stone was first extracted by the Romans more than 1,500 years ago. It was later used in medieval times to build abbeys, monasteries and, most famously, the cathedrals at Peterborough and Ely.

When quarrying stopped in about 1500, wild flowers gradually spread over the heaps of limestone rubble to create the **hotbed of wildlife** that we see today. Many unusual butterflies have been recorded here, including marbled white, chalkhill blue, brown argus and green hairstreak. There are also yellow meadow ant mounds. And if you're here on a warm summer evening, you may spot the weird green lights of the glow-worm.

Nearby Places to Visit

Just over the border in Lincolnshire, **Burghley House** is well worth a visit, and not only during the Horse Trials season. There's a family version of the house audio tour, various children's workshops and the excitingly-named 'Garden of Surprises' which, with its revolving Caesars' heads and gushing fountains, is sure to please on a hot day – but don't forget to bring a towel! www.burghley.co.uk

2

Thorney

A Model Village with Gnomes

Come on – it's this way!

L ike Nellie, a few elephants have said goodbye to the circus here. You, on the other hand, can say hello to some sports cars, a windmill, the odd swan, a collection of garden gnomes and the best cheese-on-toast in the west (probably).

Getting there *Thorney lies 7 miles east of Peterborough and 14 miles west of Wisbech. From the A47 take the B1167 exit to Thorney, driving onto Abbey Place at the crossroads, with the Rose and Crown behind you.*

Length of walk 2½ miles.
Time to allow 1–1½ hours.
Terrain A pleasant circular route, mostly off-road, with flat easy terrain and one stile. Take care near drainage ditches, cattle and seasonal nettles.
Start/Parking Abbey Place. (GR: TF 281042).
Map OS Explorer 235
Refreshments Ancarig Tea

Rooms offer a range of tasty and child-friendly options, including cheese or baked beans on toast and a host of yummy cakes.

1 Head back towards the crossroads and the Rose and Crown pub. Petrol heads in the party should detour right and choose their dream pair of wheels at the classic car showrooms – a 1967 Triumph or a 1978 MG Midget perhaps? (Kids be warned; they'd need quite a lot of pocket money.) Otherwise, turn left, crossing onto The Causeway over the bridge with a Methodist chapel on your right. Look at the village sign – how many monks are keeping watch outside Thorney Abbey? Proceed on the

◆ Fun Things to See and Do ◆

Along the riverside are clumps of what is commonly known as goose grass, sometimes called cleavers, scurvy grass or even 'sticky willie'. In the Harry Potter books, it's used in potion-making and can be bought in a Diagon Alley apothecary. In real life, it has been used as a 16th-century slimming aid, in skin disease treatment and as a substitute for coffee. Why not **imagine your own goose-grass concoctions**? Alternatively, it's an **irresistible missile**, ideal for sticking to the backs of fellow walkers. Grown-ups caught carrying a cleaver unawares for five minutes pay a forfeit by carrying the thrower on their back for five minutes.

The Walk

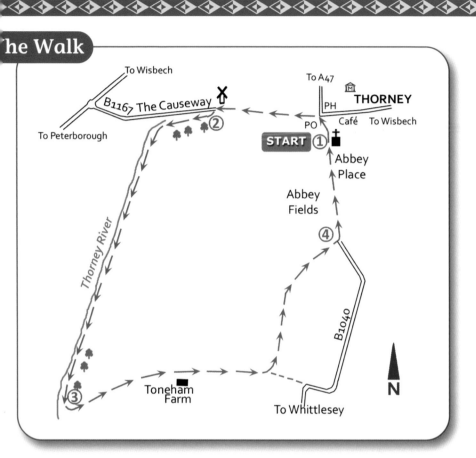

ample grass verge, checking to see the date of the windmill on your right. Continue as though leaving the village before taking the signed kissing gate to your left.

2 Now turn right along the narrow path between the trees. In summer the path is lush with cow parsley and goose grass, and in autumn there's a fine supply of conkers. Mind your heads if they're dropping! The path dips away from the road after which you tread a straight path with trees to your right, and a ditch and field to your left. Continue forwards, looking right for swans and yellow flag iris on Thorney River. Bricks to build the village of Thorney were brought along here from local pits and the River Nene. The first professional national skating championships were also held here in December 1879, won by 'Fish' Smart. Imagine skating here yourself!

3 When the tree line ends, you'll see a double-gabled house ahead and the ditch alongside curves to the left. Turn left to follow it around, onto a gravel farm track, heading towards some farm buildings. It's usually quiet but do exercise caution as you approach the farmyard. Proceed towards a long, metal gate, dipping through the gap to the left of it. On your left is an impressive garden gnome collection. Walk until you reach a pair of houses – in which year were they built? – then turn left along the signposted footpath with another ditch to the left. Head over the footbridge and stile then follow the worn grass path through the field curving gently right. If there are cattle here, walk calmly and quietly towards the wooden gate in the corner, through the kissing gate and onto the pavement opposite.

4 Turn left back towards the village, stopping if you wish to read the information board about Abbey Fields and the Thorney Wildlife Park which housed retired circus animals, including

Thorney's attractive village sign

elephants, from 1969–78. Continue past another village sign, stopping to admire the Abbey church of St Mary's and St Botolph's to the right (the date stone refers to when it was re-roofed in 1638!), and then return to your car.

Thorney

◆ Background Notes ◆

Thorney can trace its roots back to AD 500. It was originally named Ankeridge, meaning a monastery for hermits, or 'anchorites', founded here in 662. The current name of Thorney came probably from 'the isle of thorns' because of the holly, gorse and bracken growing atop what was once an island here. The monastery fell into disrepair but was rebuilt in 972 as a Benedictine abbey. At the Dissolution under Henry VIII it was stripped of building materials such as lead from the stained-glass windows. Some assets went to Cambridge to build college chapels, and the Abbey's church became a ruin.

In the 17th century, Dutchman Cornelius Vermuyden was charged with draining the fens for agricultural use. Experts from France and the Low Countries came to live in Thorney, and it became a place of many languages. Some 20,000 acres of agricultural land were eventually reclaimed and farmed by tenant farmers.

From 1849, a programme of rebuilding began, bringing Thorney to the high standards of a 'model village'. Many of the buildings are still around today not least at the Tankyard site, location of the Thorney Heritage Museum. Tel. 01733 270908; www.thorney-museum.org.uk

Nearby Places to Visit

Why not try nearby **Pigeons Farm**? There are plenty of farm-related activities like egg collecting, 'Gobots' (electric robots with secret weapons!) and a huge 'jumping pillow' on which adults and children can bounce to their heart's content! There is a café serving home-cooked food where visitors may eat without visiting the farm; www.pigeonsfarm.co.uk

Or try **Flag Fen** 'Stonehenge of the Fens' near Peterborough to find out how our ancestors lived during the Bronze Age. The summer programme includes special weekend events, craft activities, storytelling, I Spy trails and more. Tel. 01733 313414.

3

Ferry Meadows Country Park

A Ferry Nice Day Out

Just think – Roman soldiers may have passed this way!

If you like making an entrance, Ferry Meadows will suit you down to the ground – you can arrive here unconventionally by boat or steam train. But even if you come by car, there's plenty to float your imaginary boat, including a pontoon, a pyramid and a piece of history straight from your school books. Watch out, Queen Boudicca has been on the warpath hereabouts!

Ferry Meadows Country Park

Getting there *Ferry Meadows Country Park is 3 miles west of Peterborough. Leave the A1 for Peterborough on the A605 and follow the brown signs to the country park. You can also arrive by train using the Nene Valley Railway (visit www.nvr.org.uk for details of timetables and ticket prices) or boat. There are several companies that hire out craft or offer boat trips to the park, including Posh Boatz whose website and contact details are www.poshboatz.co.uk, tel. 01733 240678.*

Length of walk 2¼ miles.
Time to allow 1–1½ hours.
Terrain An easy circular route with hard-surfaced paths, perfect for buggies.

Start/Parking The visitor car park (2.1m height barrier; seasonal fee) and proceed to the visitor centre. (GR: TL 149973).
Map OS Explorer 227
Refreshments The Green Café by the visitor centre offers no-nonsense fare and children's lunch boxes. Tel. 01733 234493. Or try the licensed Lakeside Café and Bar at the Watersports Centre for food with a view – home-made meals and cakes overlooking yachts on the lake. Tel. 01733 370293. There are also several permanent barbecue stands (first come, first served) or 500 acres on which to find the perfect picnic spot.

1 Start at the visitor centre, admiring the four mature elms, VIP survivors of the tree world! Walk northwards with Overton

◆ Fun Things to See and Do ◆

With a miniature sit-on train, three separate play areas, river trips, mini-golf, fishing, duck-feeding and open space in which to cycle, walk or play, there should be plenty to keep your party out of mischief. As a starter for ten, how about a spot of **welly wanging**? (Mind other picnickers or over-friendly dogs.) The rules are simple: everyone takes off a boot and, from an agreed line, propels it as far as they can. Do change to 'shoe' or 'sandal' wanging as seasonally appropriate.

The Walk

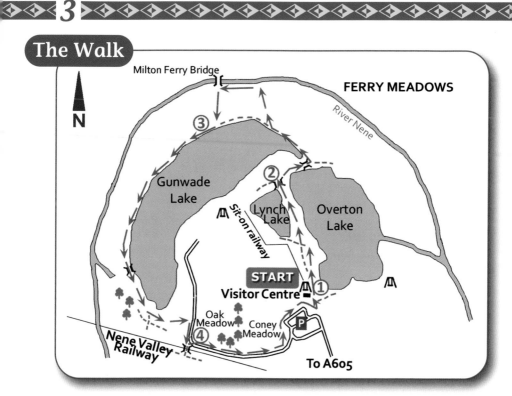

Lake on your right and the visitor centre on your left. When the path forks, go right, off the main path. You'll soon see a stone plinth which explains the early history of the site. Part of a 1st-century Roman military ditch is shown in outline and it seems that Queen Boudicca fought not far from here. Walk on as the path curves left, looking out for cormorants on the lake to your right. Stop and look at the wooden sculpture called the *Song of Sisyphus*. What do you think it looks like? When you reach a

crossroads with the main path, turn right. Lynch Lake is now on your left with Overton Lake through the trees on your right. Listen for honking geese, and do an impression!

② Cross the bridge, peering over into the still waters for water boatmen. Turn right, then cross a longer pontoon. How many different kinds of water bird can you spot? Turn left beyond the bridge and walk alongside Gunwade Lake on your left. Continue until the path forks, where you go right. On your right is Heron Meadow where you may spot some long-legged namesakes. The path bends left before the graceful River Nene and you'll soon see the majestic arches of Milton Ferry Bridge. At the T-junction, turn left, away from the bridge, heading back towards Gunwade Lake.

3 At the T-junction, turn right through a wooden gate. Wannabe Olympian yachtspersons will enjoy the boats on the lake to the left. Walk on towards the big sculpture built from Portland stone. Any guesses as to what it is? (Psst, it's actually called *The Pyramid* by John Maine.) Cross the bridge and continue with the lake still on your left. When the path bends

sharp left and meets a junction of trails, ignore the paths off right, but keep left, hugging the perimeter of the lake. Continue until you reach a fork, where you take the path to the right. At the barriers turn right, parallel to the road. As the path curves left, you'll see a brick-built bridge to the right which crosses the Nene Valley Railway.

4 Turn left, passing the metal road barriers, and carefully cross onto the tarmac path on the other side of the road. You're now on the south side of Oak Meadow. Continue along the path parallel to the road as it passes a dividing line of trees into Coney Meadow and on towards the car park and visitor centre.

Background Notes

Ferry Meadows Country Park's name derives from the ferry which took passengers and goods over the river before Milton Ferry Bridge was built in 1716. The ferry was called the Gunnerswade or Gunwade Ferry, hence the name of the largest lake created in the 1970s.

Nearby Places to Visit

The **Nene Valley Railway** is a treat for steam buffs. It runs for 7½ miles between Yarwell Junction and Peterborough, with its headquarters at Wansford station. The Ferry Meadows station is situated at the entrance to the park. Tel. 01780 784444; www.nvr.org.uk for details.

Witcham

Witcham Chips?

Racing along Bury Road

March like a Roman or chant like a witch (bring a mini-cauldron container) and stride out for a fenland walk featuring a somewhat lazy fire engine, some beautiful horses and a ten 'green' turbines song. This place is famous for peas but if it helps spur you on, the walk finishes at a pub with award-winning chips.

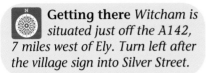

Getting there *Witcham is situated just off the A142, 7 miles west of Ely. Turn left after the village sign into Silver Street.*

Length of walk 2¾ miles.
Time to allow 1½–2 hours.
Terrain An easy, flat circular route.
Start/Parking Silver Street outside the White Horse pub. (GR: TL 462799).
Map OS Explorer 226

Refreshments The White Horse is open for lunch at weekends, and welcomes families. With real-ale accolades, a 'secret' garden and home-cooked grub, including the 'Easy Rider's Cheesy Chips' award, it's worth timing your visit to coincide. Tel. 01353 775368; www.whitehorsewitcham.co.uk

❶ With the pub behind you, walk right until you reach the crossroads. A quick detour right takes you to the Witcham village

The Walk

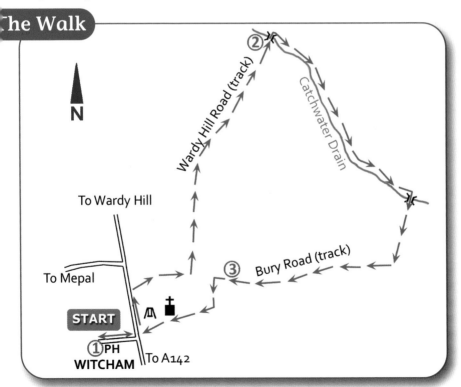

sign. Who knows what the red vehicle is? It is in fact a fire engine, used only once in its time apparently. Now about turn, back up Martin's Lane with the recreation ground on your right. Continue past a run of houses until just after The Haven, where you'll find a public byway sign towards Back Lane and Wardy Hill. Follow this grassy track towards a five-bar gate and then on to a junction, where you turn left along Wardy Hill Road. The dirt track widens to a broad, grassy path. See who finds the gap in the hedge on your right to glimpse distant Ely Cathedral. How long would it take to build a replica in Lego? On the other side, crane over the metal gate to spot the wind farms. Count the turbines or make up a song about them, *Ten Green Bottles* style!

2 The track drops gently and takes you over a ditch known as Catchwater Drain. Don't worry, it's not a smelly old pipe under a plughole but one of the many man-made waterways that crisscross the fens to keep the land dry. Turn immediately right after crossing and walk with the water on your right. The path soon sweeps right and there's another clear view of Ely Cathedral. Now look for a path to the right, back over the drain. Responsible scouts can be sent ahead to find it. Once over, you're onto Bury Road, a gently-climbing grassy lane. At the top, the lane bears right. Go through a metal gate as the grass turns into a dirt track, continuing straight ahead. Peer through the trees on your right to some dilapidated farm buildings. Perhaps the Witch of Witcham lives here? (The name actually derives from a local tree and means 'the place of the wych elms'.)

◆ Fun Things to See and Do ◆

How about making some **wand-erful witch's brew**? Fill a container with leaves, petals and anything colourful or smelly (but sanitary!) you find along the way. Look for a mixing stick and mash your ingredients together with water from the backpack. Give your potion a name and imagine what your magic mixture could do.

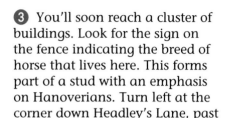

3 You'll soon reach a cluster of buildings. Look for the sign on the fence indicating the breed of horse that lives here. This forms part of a stud with an emphasis on Hanoverians. Turn left at the corner down Headley's Lane, past Sharmer House. At Witcham House, turn right onto the footpath which takes you back along the High Street. After the church and the hall, you'll come up alongside the recreation ground on your right. Second time around, do run over and have a go on the swings! When finished, go over the crossroads into Silver Street and back to your car.

Background Notes ◆

Flint and axes from Neolithic farmers have been found here, proving the area was settled over 6,000 years ago. Bronze Age folk left spearheads, daggers and shields. And from the Romans, coins have been unearthed, and a splendid helmet (circa AD 14) which is now in the British Museum.

These days, Witcham is host to the World Pea Shooting Championships, held here annually since 1971. Originally started as a village hall fund-raiser by a local headmaster, the event now welcomes pea shooters from all over the world. The trophy is hotly contested, and competitors have used lasers, gyroscopic balancing systems and even bits borrowed from a son's Nintendo to create their very own weapons of mass pea-struction!

Nearby Places to Visit

Witcham was on an island before the low-lying fens were drained to create farmland 400 years ago. Budding engineers should visit **Prickwillow Engine Museum** to find out how it was done. Tel. 01353 688360; www.prickwillow-engine-museum.co.uk

At the **Mepal Outdoor Centre**, there's adventure play, kayaking, pedal karts, a 'Scramble Zone' for climbers and zorbing. There's also a café. Tel. 01354 692251; www.mepal.co.uk

5

Upwood

Don't Get Ants in Your Pants

Hopping over ant hillocks

If you're keen to feast your eyes on fungi, this is the autumn walk for you (although you'd be wise to feast only on those from a shop). If you are here in the spring, then all is not lost as you'll be treated to the sight of bluebells aplenty and the rare green-winged orchid. Whatever the time of year, you're sure to enjoy an encounter with the amazing Upwood Meadows ant hillocks. Just take care not to get any ants in your pants, or perhaps down the top of your wellington boots!

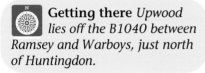 **Getting there** *Upwood lies off the B1040 between Ramsey and Warboys, just north of Huntingdon.*

Length of walk 3 miles.
Time to allow 2 hours.
Terrain Flat but best without a buggy. Take boots if it has been wet.
Starting/Parking The High Street opposite the Cross Keys pub. (GR: TL 259827)
Map OS Explorer 227.
Refreshments The Cross Keys is a family-friendly village local, with a tree-trunk slide in the huge garden, friendly staff and a good-value children's menu. Tel. 01487 813384; www.crosskeysupwood.co.uk

❶ Walk north up the High Street with the pub on your right. Turn left down the narrow signposted alleyway opposite number 21. At the wooden fence turn right, then left at the field corner, walking with the hedge on your left. Proceed through the gap in the hedge and along the side of the field for roughly 200 yards. Upon reaching a white country walks sign, turn right, taking the path which veers diagonally across the field. Take a moment to enjoy the sweeping view.

❷ At the hedge, turn left onto Turf Fen Road. Walk for some distance along this chalky track, looking out for Lady's Wood on your distant left. Ignore the field openings to your left, but continue along a row of bushes until you are level with a lone oak to your right, turning left only when you get to a red and white striped post onto a clear farm track. Keep on this path as it wriggles right, then left, drawing

◆ Fun Things to See and Do ◆

 **Become a photographer** for the day with a digital camera or a disposable one. Look around for great photo opportunities – your dog wading through bluebells, big sis looking cross-eyed at a fungi, dad balancing one-footed on an ant hill – and take as many as you can. Print the pictures afterwards and make an album.

Kiddiwalks in Cambridgeshire

The Walk

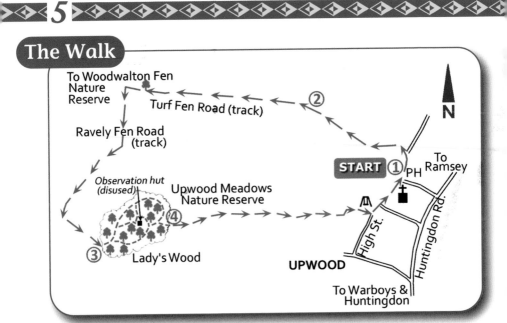

alongside the wood on your left. Continue forward until you meet a ditch and a small clump of trees, with a telegraph pole ahead. Turn left now, heading towards the wood, passing another striped gas marker and walking parallel to the overhead wires. Bear right at the end to find the tucked-away and signposted entrance to the nature reserve.

3 Once inside, the adventurous can explore the wood at will; there are three main paths, none of which are very long which will take you through to the other side. The easiest way to avoid getting lost, however, is via the long perimeter path, taking the left option at a series of four forks. This will eventually take you through a small gap in the hedge onto the corner of an open field.

4 Walk straight ahead with the hedge to your left, continuing to a wooden bridge and gate. Take the middle path through the hummocky ant-hill meadow. Follow the path through two further gates, across an open field, emerging after a kissing gate next to a bungalow. Turn left and follow the cul-de-sac to the end where a small path takes you past a children's playground. At the road, turn left opposite the village hall to return to your starting point.

Background Notes ◆

Lady's Wood is part of the ancient woodland that once covered most of East Anglia. The dead wood and fallen trees from this once-managed coppice provide the perfect habitat for insects and fungi. Amongst the surviving trees are oak, ash and maple, several large crab apples, hawthorns and English elm.

In spring you'll find a sea of bluebells mixed with white star-like stitchwort. You might spot lesser celandine with its yellow flowers and heart-shaped leaves. Close your eyes and search out some ransoms, aka bear's garlic (*allium ursinum*). While you won't find any actual bears in Lady's Wood, if you sniff the air in spring you might smell the ramsons' characteristic garlic-like scent.

At **Upwood Meadows** you can see the ancient ridges and furrows made by ox-drawn ploughs during the 17th century. This is also where you'll spot the large hillocks formed by the yellow meadow ant, as well as a colourful array of grassland herbs such as cowslips, saw-wort and great burnet, and last but not least the VIP colony of green-winged orchids which flower in May.

Nearby Places to Visit

Further north is **Woodwalton Fen**, one of Britain's oldest nature reserves established in 1910 by the banker and amateur naturalist Charles Rothschild. With its network of water-filled ditches and abundant wildlife, it's a fascinating place showing what the fens were like before drainage brought the land to its current level. Visit www.wildlifebcnp.org for more information.

To see what life used to be like in a small fenland community, call into the seasonally open **Ramsey Farm Museum**. Tel 01487 815715; www.ramseyruralmuseum.co.uk.

Aversley Wood, Sawtry

Take a Bough

Well, we're here! Let's get going

Wannabe Tarzans will holler with delight at the vine-dripping trees and real-life deer to track. But if Tarzan's (or Jane's) jungle skills fail to sniff out any genuine animals, why not follow in the footsteps of medieval farmers, herding your flock of grown-ups out front? Marks out of ten for the best animal impressions!

Getting there *Leave the A1(M) at junction 15, exit the roundabout signposted to Sawtry, then take the third road to your left, St Judith's Lane. The car park is at the end before the road turns 90° left.*

Length of walk 3 miles.
Time to allow 2 hours.
Terrain All off-road, grassy and undulating woodland paths. A steep hike to reach the wood which can be boggy in winter.
Start/Parking The St Judith's Lane car park in Sawtry. (GR: TL 170828).
Map OS Explorer 227
Refreshments Tilly's Coffee Shop is a welcoming, spotless café, with a soft play area for smaller children, family-friendly food and a take-away service for picnics. Turn left out of St Judith's Lane to find the café next to the fire station. Tel. 01487 831200.

1 Head over the stile just beyond the information board and cross over into St Judith's Field. Bear left, aiming for the path heading uphill with allotments to your left and a hedgerow to your right. After a steep climb, go through the wooden kissing gate then continue, still climbing, with a hedgerow to your right. At the brow of the hill, there's a seasonal boggy patch which the brave can squelch through. Otherwise scramble up and

◆ Fun Things to See and Do ◆

If it's a blustery autumn day, why not try **catching wishes**? As you walk through the woods, see who can catch a leaf as it falls to the ground. Careful the wind doesn't snatch your prize away! Those skilful or lucky enough to catch one can make a wish.

Or try **blindfold adventuring**! Tie on a hankie or similar as a blindfold around the first adventurer (or shut your eyes tight instead). Nominate a 'guide dog' to lead them carefully around obstructions, getting them to touch, hear and smell the things around. Make up stories about what you find.

The Walk

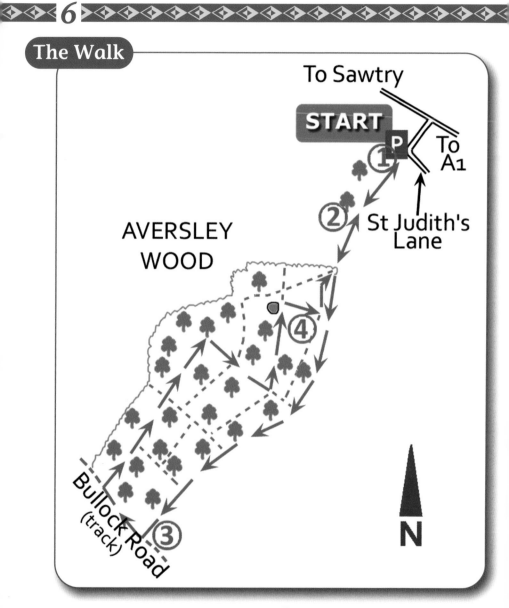

To Sawtry

START

P

To A1

1

2 St Judith's Lane

AVERSLEY WOOD

4

Bullock Road (track)

3

N

around the bushes to your right in order to avoid the goo.

❷ Continue straight on. As the path starts to go downhill, you will see the wood coming up on

Inspecting the pond at point 3 of the walk

your right. Resist the urge to turn into it but proceed along its edge, over a two-lane footbridge with open fields to your left. Keep going all the way along until you reach a wooden memorial bench at a T-junction at the corner of the wood. You have now reached Bullock Road which forms the south-western edge of Aversley Wood.

❸ Turn right onto the broad grassy path, with the wood on your right and fields to your left. Continue until you reach a five-bar gate with a Woodland Trust sign to your right. Enter on the woodland path, slipping around (or over!) the gate. Ignore the first two right-hand paths, taking the third turn-off down a rolling embankment which swoops down, then up – this is zooming ahead of the grown-ups territory! At a crossroads and bench, turn left, proceeding downhill. Continue until you reach a glade with a raised pond to the left. Walk up the steps to inspect it.

❹ When you've had your fill, take a right turn back towards the track you walked in on. You can either dip off left 30 yards before the information board, snaking

Kiddiwalks in Cambridgeshire

your way up to the corner of the wood, or leave the wood immediately at the end of this straight path. In both cases, turn left and retrace your earlier steps along the field-side path. After the kissing gate and before the allotments, you could cross the wooden bridge to your left onto the large recreational field; great for ball games, kites and picnics. The car park is in the bottom right-hand corner.

◆ Background Notes ◆

Cambridgeshire holds the title of England's least-wooded county which makes **Aversley Wood** all the more special. At more than 150 acres, it is one of Cambridgeshire's largest ancient woodland sites, dating back to the Ice Age and mentioned in the Domesday Book. Jogging forward a little, you can see evidence of past cultivation with ridge and furrow lines thought to date from around 1350 after which the Black Death diminished the population, the land was abandoned and it reverted to woodland. The size and shape of the wood you see today dates from 1768, and the internal ride system from 1887, around which time large-scale coppicing was stopped.

With its sunny open rides and damp shady places it is now a haven for thousands of wildlife species. Growing aplenty here are bluebells, dewberry, dog's mercury, common spotted orchid and the intriguingly-named enchanter's nightshade. The wood is also home to twelve species of butterfly – notably black hairstreak, white admiral and white letter hairstreak – and at least 37 species of bird. Look out also for the muntjac deer.

Nearby Places to Visit

Hamerton Park Zoo is a fifteen-minute ride from Sawtry. Opened in 1990 as a conservation sanctuary, the zoo has 15 acres of parkland with an array of creatures from around the world. Children can enjoy the 'Stroll-a-Safari', as well as two good play areas, an enclosed picnic garden and a coffee shop. Tel. 01832 293362; www.hamertonzoopark.com

7

Hinchingbrooke Country Park

What's Going on Here Den?

Puppy love in Bob's Wood

Dog-owners will feel at home, but if you don't have one just observe; it's great here for Cutest Dog Spotting competitions. Likewise, if you don't have a pet caterpillar, don't worry. Pop over to the mini-beast mansion, perfect for Get Everybody Itchy competitions – make your fingers do the walking up each others' backs. Otherwise, get ready for some pond-dipping, conker collecting or den building. Sounds like bags of fun!

Kiddiwalks in Cambridgeshire

Getting there
Hinchingbrooke Country Park is in west Huntingdon. Leave the A14 at junction 22, taking the B1514 to Huntingdon and follow the brown Country Park signs.

Length of walk 2¼ miles.
Time to allow 1½ hours.
Terrain An easy route with maintained paths, usually fine for a buggy although the woodland paths can get muddy in winter. Some unfenced water.
Start/Parking Use the country park car park (fee payable). (GR: TL 221716)

Map OS Explorer 225
Refreshments Hot and cold food is served at the visitor centre café, or aspiring chefs can try one of the permanent barbecue stands. Just around the corner is the Brampton Mill pub where you can see the water wheel in action and eat posh pizzas in the riverside seating area. Tel: 01480 459758 or visit www.thebramptonmill.co.uk

1 Walk into Bob's Wood signposted from the top of the car park. Gather your den-building fodder here, or try balancing along the fallen trunks. At the crossroads, go through the gate

◆ Fun Things to See and Do ◆

Why not **create an elf den**? Look for a good spot around a large fallen log or leaning tree. Make an apex with three or more sturdy twigs, then thread smaller sticks, ferns and leaf litter around to make a shelter. Make a door, a chimney and a garden, and think up a good address. Older kids can make a full-size den, using larger fallen branches in Bob's Wood. For safety, adults should scavenge material from existing dens, and carefully dismantle your masterpiece at the end.

Nets for **pond-dipping** can be borrowed from the café for a small fee (to prevent spread of disease please don't use your own). Or on summer Sundays, **visit the apiary**, where you can meet the bee keeper and his charges, if they're not too grumpy because of the rain that is!

The Walk

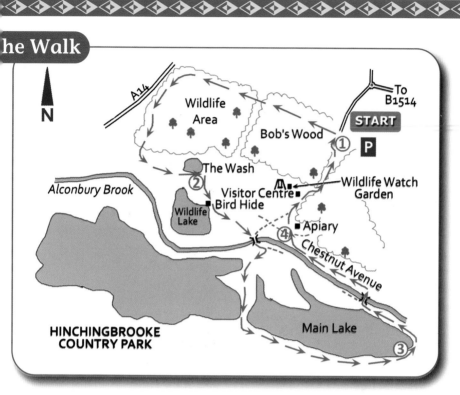

ahead and walk on. Eventually, the path turns 90° left, with road noise through the trees to your right. Meander downhill, through an open gateway. Keep to the main path until emerging onto an open area. Turn left, the distant visitor centre ahead, and a post and wire fence on your right. Continue past the small bulrush pond to your left known as The Wash. Junior fishermen can try pond-dipping here. At the T-junction beyond, you could detour briefly left – see who crests the sandy mounds and shouts 'king of the castle!' first.

❷ Returning to the T-junction, turn right onto the left-curving path which brings the Wildlife Lake up onto your right. Check out the bird hide identification charts. Who can spot some wildfowl? Anyone see a chicken? Rejoin the path, dipping under tree cover as it curves right. Play musical tree trunks – each trying to find your own seat – then swing sharp left towards a T-junction, turning right to cross the bridge. At the third bench, follow the gravel path right. Walk between two belts of water turning left at the end, keeping Main Lake on your left. Count the benches around the water or try a Three Billy Goats Gruff re-enactment at the boardwalk halfway along.

❸ At the end, the path swings left, then rebounds round with Main Lake still on your left and Alconbury Brook on your right. Why not find a fat blade of grass, stretch it between your thumbs and see who can make it whistle? You'll soon reach the Water Sports Centre and an open area with a picnic bench and little jetty – a favourite dipping spot for local dogs. Turn right from here over the arched bridge, then left onto the majestic Chestnut Avenue.

❹ At the avenue's end, follow the main path right, walking alongside a twined branch fence on your left. The apiary is on your right; read the inscription on the bench. To your left are barbecue stands and gym equipment if anyone fancies stopping off to improve their muscle tone. The alluring red slide, zip wire and café ahead might just prove more appealing however! Check out the adjacent Wildlife Watch Garden. When you're done, cross the zebra by the visitor centre and turn left through the trees to the car park.

◆ Background Notes ◆

Today's country park was once part of the Hinchingbrooke House estate. The house is now a school although you can visit it on summer Sundays. Tel: 01480 375678. The building is mostly Tudor but there are remains of a 13th-century nunnery within the walls. After the dissolution of the monasteries by Henry VIII, the Hinchingbrooke estate was given to the Cromwell family in 1538. As well as entertaining royalty – Queen Elizabeth I and King James I both visited.

Nearby Places to Visit
Bangers and mash fans should detour to **Johnsons of Old Hurst** who make 18 varieties of sausages. Patrons of the Eccentric Englishman tea room and farm shop can use the children's playing field with toy tractors and fort. Tel: 01487 824658; www.johnsonsofoldhurst.co.uk

8

Houghton Meadow

A Magical Meadow Meander

Feeding the ducks at the mill pond

First off, fit in with the locals and say 'Hoeton' (like the garden tool) not 'Howton'. Now get set to walk past an abandoned railway, a church spire that went AWOL and a working water mill once used for after-dark sleepovers. There's a busy lock, the chance to go punting and a whiff of magic as you cross flood meadows where *The Children of Green Knowe* was set. Enchanting stuff!

8

Getting there *Leave the A14 at junction 25 towards Hemingford Abbots. Drive down Common Lane, left off the High Street, turn right into Meadow Lane and park by the footbridge.*

Length of walk 3½ miles.
Time to allow 2 hours.
Terrain Flat, easy terrain but a couple of stiles and can be wet underfoot. Open water and a lane with occasional traffic so watch youngsters.

Start/Parking Meadow Lane next to the footbridge. (GR: TL 277714)
Map OS Explorer 225.
Refreshments The Axe and Compass in Hemingford Abbots is a 15th-century thatched pub, with a warm welcome for families. There's a beer garden with children's play area, kids' menu, baby-changing facilities and a sunny-weekends tuck shop serving sweets and ice creams. Tel. 01480 463605; www.axeandcompass.co.uk . Alternatively, try Houghton

◆ Fun Things to See and Do ◆

This walk crosses flood meadows – grass fields near a river that occasionally flood in winter. The main character in the *The Children of Green Knowe* by Lucy Boston is a 7-year-old boy called Tolly who first arrives here when it's flooded and dark. Imagine the excitement! Ask a grown-up about their **favourite book** from childhood – the characters, setting and plot. Tell them about your favourite book too.

Willow trees grow along the banks of the River Ouse here. They used to be regularly cut back so that grazing animals couldn't eat them, and the harvested wood was used for thatching, basket making and fencing. Perhaps you could **make your own stick weaving**? Find a forked stick, zigzagging some string across it to make a web. Collect grasses, feathers and winged seeds and weave them into your creation to make – ta da – your very own Houghton Meadow dream catcher.

he Walk

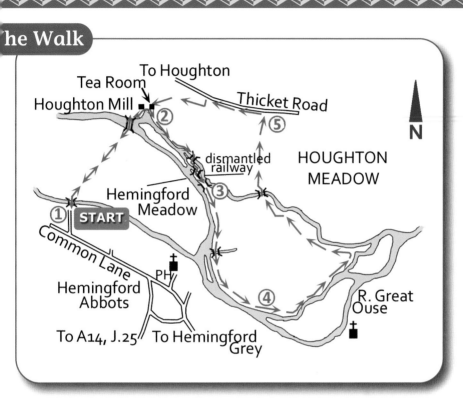

To Houghton

Tea Room

Houghton Mill

Thicket Road

② ⑤

N

dismantled railway

HOUGHTON MEADOW

Hemingford Meadow ③

① START

Common Lane

PH

Hemingford Abbots

To A14, J.25 / To Hemingford Grey

④

R. Great Ouse

scones in the National Trust tea room. Seasonal opening. Tel. 01480 301494.

❶ Cross the bridge and go through the pedestrian gate ignoring the Private Property sign; this is a well-used right of way. Follow the footpath across Hemingford Meadow, through another gate and onto the bridge. It is almost impossible *not* to stop here awhile to watch the boats negotiate the locks. Continue as the path snakes around into the cover of trees past a huddle of crust-hungry ducks and the chance to hire a punt in summer. Go under the archway through Houghton Mill – how many windows can you see? – and right at the end towards the National Trust tea room.

❷ Veer right, around the tea room, keeping close to the banks of the mill pond on your right. Continue with the campsite on your left then through a kissing gate. Follow the path past a

A tree-climbing opportunity beside the River Great Ouse

bubbling weir and over four footbridges, camping up the 'who's that trip-trapping over my bridge?' theatricals as you see fit. At the bridge over Gull Weir you could try a turn at Pooh sticks. Before climbing over the stile at the end of the 4th footbridge there are also the remains of a railway bridge to look at – the old St Ives to Kettering line which closed in 1959.

❸ The path now follows the banks of the River Great Ouse through a series of meadows, past

Hemingford Abbots church and over another footbridge. After the island in the river – who can imagine setting up camp there? – continue past another weir, heading for the stile between the trees. On the other side, you'll see Hemingford Grey church tower immediately ahead. The steeple was blown off in a great storm in 1741, and locals say that it is now lurking in the murky depths below!

❹ Follow the curve of the river as it bends slowly left until you meet a tributary coming in from the left just ahead of a rusty fence. Turn left here doubling back across the top edge on the meadow, sticking close to the water on your right. Go through the weighted gate at the end, over the bridge to your right and along a tree-lined track. Who can spot the route of the disused railway?

5 At the end, turn left down pretty Thicket Road. It's a quiet dead-end lane but do listen for traffic. Just before a Narnia lamp post, count the tall chimneys on the house ahead, then turn left down a public footpath. Follow it as it turns right with a fence and then a wall on your right-hand side. Proceed until another public footpath sign invites you to walk diagonally left past the campsite towards the tea room and mill. From here, retrace your steps back towards the lock-bridge, across the meadow to your car.

Background Notes ◆

Houghton Mill is the last working watermill on the Great Ouse, though not too long ago you could sleep there as it used to be a Youth Hostel. Today it's well worth a visit with great hands-on activities and a 'Cat and Rat' children's trail around the mill. There are milling demonstrations on Sundays and a family events programme including hands-on baking days. Tel: 01480 301494; www.nationaltrust.org.uk/main/w-houghtonmill

Nearby Places to Visit

You can visit **The Manor at Hemingford Grey** to see the house in which *The Children of Green Knowe* was set, and buy the books. Built in the 1130s The Manor is one of the oldest continuously inhabited houses in Britain. Inside there's a wealth of treasures including a mesmerizing rocking horse, a dizzyingly tall chimney stack and a very special mouse. With a moated garden, life-size topiary chess pieces and an enormous gramophone trumpet, a visit here is nothing short of a delight. Visits to the house are strictly by prior appointment although the garden can be seen without an appointment. Tel 01480 463134: www.greenknowe.co.uk

Kimbolton

Follies and Fireworks

Who's going to get there first?

A haunted castle, a deserted folly and the whiff of some Henry VIII history – how cool is that? There's also a café with dangerously great cakes, a Pooh sticks bridge, hungry ducks, and you might even catch a fair. What's more, Kimbolton is famous for fireworks, so don't forget to glance up occasionally to watch for any overhead. You never know, it might just be a testing day. BANG!

Getting there *Kimbolton is 7 miles west of St Neots on the B645, or leave the A14 at exit 16 onto the B660, turning left at the T-junction into Kimbolton village.*

Length of walk 2¾ miles.
Time to allow 1–1½ hours.
Terrain A moderate figure of eight including an option to shorten. Some field walking and gentle climbs so best without buggies.
Start/Parking Kimbolton High Street. (GR: TL 099677).
Map OS Explorer 225
Refreshments The New Sun Inn (tel. 01480 860052) and Buttercups café (tel. 01489

861000) both get a serious thumbs up – the latter has wonderful sticky buns! Alternatively, if you're looking for a friendly pub with swings and slides, drive west to Tilbrook where you'll get a warm welcome at the White Horse. Tel. 01480 860764; www.whitehorsetilbrook.com

1 Walk to Watsons Electrical shop on the High Street. Pass through the 'secret passageway' entrance to the right of the door. (Six-footer adults, mind your heads!) Turn right into East Street and then left at the end past Abingtons, formerly the town workhouse. Follow the path around, then turn left over the

Fun Things to See and Do ◆

Fans of Guy Fawkes' night will be thrilled to hear that the village is famous for fireworks. The founder of Kimbolton Fireworks, a clergyman and former master at the school, is known affectionately as the 'Master Blaster Pastor'. Why not collect twigs, grasses and fallen leaves of different colours along the way? At the end, lay your booty on the ground to **create a fizzing fireworks picture**. Or take inspiration from Warren House. Originally home to the warrener – a man paid to manage rabbits for their meat and fur – it was given a new façade in the 18th-century to create a view from Kimbolton Castle. Take turns **describing your own perfect folly** – the wackier the better!

9

The Walk

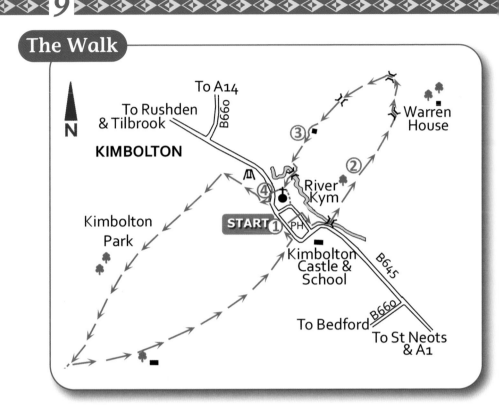

To A14

To Rushden & Tilbrook

B660

N

KIMBOLTON

③

Warren House

②

River Kym

④

Kimbolton Park

START ① PH

Kimbolton Castle & School

B645

To Bedford B660

To St Neots & A1

---

small bridge across the River Kym. Proceed straight onwards, ignoring the options to turn left. As you walk up the tree-lined grassy path, peek through the hedgerow to your right. See who spots Warren House, the folly that can be seen from the castle.

❷ After emerging from the trees start the gentle ascent, turning left over the small footbridge about halfway up. Take the diagonal path up through the crops. In between Grand Old

Duke of Yorking, look back to admire the view of the castle. At the top, before the path curves gently round, take a sharp 90° left towards a gap in the hedgerow. Dip down and 'walk the planks' over a ditch before taking the path diagonally down through the field and over another footbridge towards the village.

❸ Pass the white house at the bottom, turning left beyond it and then almost immediately right onto a footpath parallel to

Trekking through a corn field

the cemetery. At the end, turn left where there's a bench, a huddle of ever-hungry ducks and a well-fenced bridge to try some gentle Pooh sticks. Cross the bridge and snake onwards through the cluster of houses until you reach the main road, watching out for traffic. (Wearier walkers can cut through the churchyard left, back onto East Street and up the passageway whence you came, right after number 19.)

④ Cross the road, walking straight on, and into Grass Yard signposted right. At the fork, turn right past the Old School House. Who can see the old bell? Walk along the alley past the playground, turning left at the end. Cross over and walk up Pound Lane. About halfway up the hill, look over your shoulder to spot Warren House again. At the top, take the sharp left signposted footpath which takes you through the field towards a tall oak tree. Can you put your arms around it? Head now back down the hill towards the castle and school buildings. Pass through the gap in the fence and follow the yellow arrows, left of the tree ahead, which mark the public footpath. Head out of the school gates and back onto the High Street.

◆ Background Notes ◆

Kimbolton is brimming with history. King Harold, he of arrow-in-eye fame, is believed to have worshipped here, and in the 1200s permission for the staging of a regular market and fair was granted by the king. This was when the current village layout was devised, with its broad High Street and quirky 90° turns in the road – a real challenge for 21st-century buses and lorries! Though there's no longer a regular market, if you visit on the third Wednesday of September you'll find the still-going-strong annual Statutory Fair. The main street is closed to traffic to make way for a good old-fashioned funfair known locally as the **Statty Fair**.

Kimbolton Castle has medieval origins but the current mansion was built largely between 1690 and 1720. It was designed by Vanbrugh and Hawksmoor, well-known architects of the period who had previously worked together at Blenheim Palace. There is also a Robert Adam gatehouse and impressive interior wall paintings by Pellegrini. The castle's most famous resident, Katharine of Aragon, died here after a period of imprisonment in 1536. Some say she haunts the building still. As floor levels have changed since her day, her ghostly torso is spookily said to glide through the floorboards whilst her legs are seen on the ceiling below! The castle, now owned by Kimbolton School, can be visited at certain times. Tel: 01480 860505; www.kimbolton.cambs.sch.uk/page/?pid=77

Nearby Places to Visit
At **Grafham Water** there's a 10-mile circuit to walk or cycle around – do as much or as little as you like. There are bikes for hire, a visitor centre, playground, gift shop and café in the Marlow car park. Tel. 01480 812154.

10

Wicken

Only Adventurers Need Apply

Time for a photo shoot at Monk's Lode

Who could resist the call to explore a place called Adventurers' Fen? With snakes at your feet, a dragonfly hotel and tales of ghostly monks, what more could a young adventurer want? But if you don't fancy yourself as Indiana Jones, why not don your explorer's hat and pull out a magnifying glass? On this walk you're following in the footsteps of a rather eminent Victorian naturalist. (That's someone into wildlife, not taking their clothes off if anyone asks!)

Kiddiwalks in Cambridgeshire

10

Getting there *Wicken is 17 miles north-east of the A10 from Cambridge, and 3 miles west of Soham, off the A1123.*

Length of walk 2¼ miles.
Time to allow 1–1½ hours.
Terrain Mostly flat, gravel tracks. Some unfenced water and a short stretch along a lane. Fine with a robust buggy although you'll need to lift it over a kissing gate.
Start/Parking The Maid's Head pub car park or on the High Street nearby. (GR: TL 571706).

Map OS Explorer 226
Refreshments The Maid's Head offers a sympathetic children's menu, as well as highly recommendable grown-up nosh, and there's a slide in the garden for any unspent energy.
Tel. 01353 720727,
www.maidsheadwicken.com.
Otherwise, try the café at the National Trust visitor centre which promises home-made cakes and the local soup known as 'fen docky'.

1 Walk east up the High Street, leaving the pub behind and to

◆ Fun Things to See and Do ◆

The Wicken village sign proudly sports a butterfly. Up to 1,000 species of moth and butterfly live in the fens today whilst Charles Darwin himself collected bugs and butterflies on sedge boats here while studying at Cambridge in the 1820s. Why not think how you would **illustrate a new sign** for Wicken using images of the animals, plants and buildings you spot on your walk. Alternatively, why not think up a funky sign for the place that you come from?

You'll pass **Fen Cottage** en route which recreates how fenlanders of yore lived. See who in your party would fancy eel stew for lunch! Do also pop into the **Dragonfly Centre** in summer to find out how dragonflies eat sideways and extend their jaws, or you could even join a dragonfly safari. Open 11 am to 4 pm at weekends from mid May to late September. Free entry. www.dragonflyproject.org.uk

The Walk

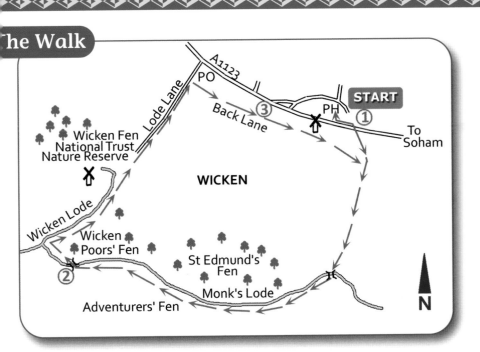

your left. Pass the Wicken butterfly village sign and turn right into Cross Green following the public footpath and Wicken Walks signs. See who spots the dovecote on your left. After Wrights Motors the lane curves right. Follow it onto the gravel track straight ahead. Walk until you reach two bridges, continuing until the second green-fenced one on your left. Take a straw poll to check everyone's feeling adventurous before crossing to the National Trust Adventurers' Fen sign. Now turn right with the waterway, a drainage channel known as Monk's Lode, on your

right. The ones who agreed to be adventurous should stop here and listen. It's said that at nearby Spinney Abbey Farm there was once an old priory and that monks can still be heard chanting across the fens in the still of the night! Continue along the water's edge which bends slowly to the right. Ignore the left turn over cattle grids, but keep walking alongside the water, minding out for peaty mole hills.

2 You eventually come to a broad flat bridge on your right which you should cross. Turn left on the other side and then almost immediately right as the path bends with the waterway. The drain on your left is called Wicken Lode, and there's a wind pump on the other bank. Walk further until you reach a windmill and the hexagon-shaped National Trust visitor centre. After any café or loo stops, proceed along the tarmac road, past Fen Cottage and the Dragonfly Centre. Take care now as you pass the National Trust car park, walking on the grass verge where possible, past a row of cottages until you reach Back Lane on your right.

3 The tarmac road soon narrows and turns into a grassy track. There are houses on your left and an open field to the right. Keep going along this alleyway until you reach a wooden kissing gate. At this point you are alongside another windmill, occasionally open to visitors and accessible from the High Street. Continue along the field edge until you reach an opening to your left and a public footpath sign pointing the way you've just come from. Turn left into the opening and retrace your steps back to the start.

◆ Background Notes ◆

Wicken Fen is the National Trust's oldest nature reserve. It shows how East Anglia would have looked in the past; a wilderness bursting with mammals, birds, plants and insects. Young ornithologists could look for a tawny owl, kestrel or perhaps a red kite. Closer to the ground, you may see an otter, or the hardy Konig ponies which are here to graze the land. And if you're lucky you might even see a grass snake at your feet – don't worry, they are harmless!

Nearby Places to Visit

If you have time to divert to Cambridge, do pop into the **Museum of Zoology** which houses a huge variety of recent and fossilized animals. Amongst them is a fabulous collection of moths and butterflies found at Wicken Fen, and beetles collected by Charles Darwin. For families there are regularly changing self-led trails; plenty to keep curious minds busy on a wet day. Best of all, it's free. www.museum.zoo.cam.ac.uk

11

Milton Country Park

Paradise Found

Where are the fish, then?

Monster-sized carp and abandoned machinery lurking in the depths of the old gravel pit lakes; this sounds like a ghostly Scooby Doo location! Fear not, there's plenty above water to keep the shivers away including ducks and swans to feed, a sun clock, two playgrounds and open spaces galore. On a sunny weekend, you could spend all day here. Just make sure you're gone before dark ...

Kiddiwalks in Cambridgeshire

Getting there *Milton Country Park lies just north of Cambridge. Leave the A10/A14 at junction 33, following the brown signs to Milton, turning right opposite Tesco through an industrial estate to the park.*

Length of walk 1¼ miles.
Time to allow Up to 1 hour.
Terrain A short, easy walk on established paths, all suitable for buggies.
Start/Parking Use the Milton Country Park car park; fee paying. (GR: TL 476620).
Map OS Explorer 226
Refreshments Café Diem is a good on-site café with toasties, soup, baked potatoes, smoothies and ice-cream. Outside, there's a panoramic, fenced-off seating area. You can also buy bags of seed here to feed the swans and ducks. Tel: 01223 425231.

1 Head into the park, with the information board and toilets on your right. At the crossroads turn left towards the visitor centre. Look for the whiteboard listing wildlife sightings. Turn left between the Sustainable and Sensory gardens, detouring inside to rub the different leaves and smell your fingers. Continue until a wooden bridge turns you 90° right. The lake in front is called Todd's Pit, a flooded gravel pit with some rather large carp skulking in the depths. Turn left, then right, around the corner

◆ Fun Things to See and Do ◆

Test the sun clock by standing on the current month marker on the central stones and seeing where your shadow falls. It's not digital technology but it's lots of fun!

Plan a special garden inspired by those here. The Sensory Garden is full of flowers and herbs chosen for their smell and touch. What would you put in your 'tang and texture' garden? Or there's the Sustainable Garden, planted with organic fruit, vegetables and flowers to show how much you can grow at home no matter what size your garden is. What would you grow? (Definitely no cabbages!)

The Walk

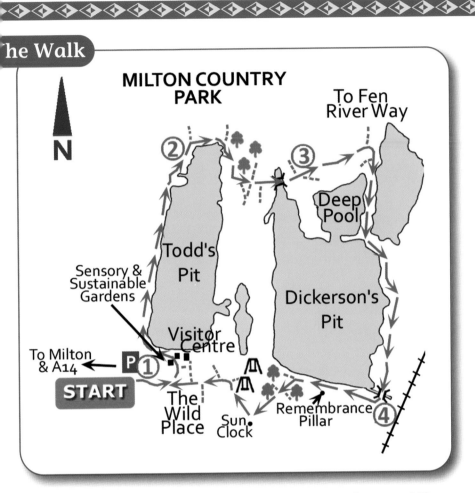

MILTON COUNTRY PARK

N

To Fen
River Way

② ③

Deep
Pool

Todd's
Pit

Sensory &
Sustainable
Gardens

Dickerson's
Pit

Visitor
Centre

To Milton
& A14

P ①

START

The
Wild
Place

Sun
Clock

Remembrance
Pillar

④

onto a wood-chip path, with the lake now on your right. Pick and scoff blackberries in season, or check each numbered fishing deck along the water's edge – are the numbers all there?

② Ignore the small trail right, keeping on the main gravelly track past another entrance from the left and a 'Welcome to Milton Country Park' sign on your right. Keep to the main route along the perimeter of the lake, ignoring minor paths left and right, until you reach a kingfisher-crested sign at a crossroads. Go straight over towards the blue-railed bridge which takes you over Dickerson's Pit. This is another

The time by the sun clock is

flooded gravel pit populated by 'silver' fish (distant cousins perhaps of the goldfish?) including chub, roach and pike. It's the shallowest lake in the park and during dry summers in years past, people waded across it. (This is no longer allowed, if any young adventurers are wondering!).

❸ At the crossroads, walk straight on until you reach a T-junction. Turning left here takes you towards the River Cam and Fen River Way, but for this walk turn right. On your right is Deep Pool which, as it says on the tin, is the deepest pit of the old gravel workings, a popular place to swim in days of yore. Some say there's still old machinery lying in the waters below. What do you think might be down there? When you reach a bench at a T-junction, turn left to follow the bicycle path arrow. You're now walking along the perimeter of Dickerson's Pit again. Keep going until you get to a wooden bridge. Afterwards, look left. Which trainspotter sees the

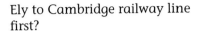

Ely to Cambridge railway line first?

4 When you reach a fork, turn right following the bike arrow. You soon emerge into an open area, the Remembrance Meadow, which centres on a memorial pillar commemorating the end of the Second World War. Try reading the inscription by walking round and round it – who ends up feeling dizzy? Continue along the path veering left onto the grass opposite a bench and wooden bridge on your right. Take the right-hand path out of the clearing through bushes and trees, and out into another glade. On your left is the raised sun clock – have a go at reading the time if it's not too cloudy. Head now towards the play area, trying out the irresistible 'whirly woks', then take the main path to the left. The Wild Place on your left is only for pre-booked educational groups, but do peer in to spot the wigwams. Then continue straight ahead to the car park to complete the circuit.

Background Notes ◆

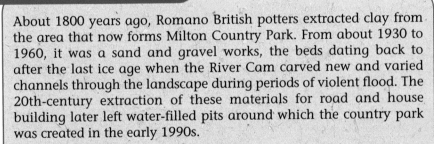

About 1800 years ago, Romano British potters extracted clay from the area that now forms Milton Country Park. From about 1930 to 1960, it was a sand and gravel works, the beds dating back to after the last ice age when the River Cam carved new and varied channels through the landscape during periods of violent flood. The 20th-century extraction of these materials for road and house building later left water-filled pits around which the country park was created in the early 1990s.

Nearby Places to Visit

Why not try the **Milton Maize Maze**, a 7-acre labyrinth with hidden clues and observation bridges. For the littlies there's also a mini maze. Outside maize season, there's plenty more, including a strawberry-loving pig called Lulu, tractor trails, go-karts and hungry rainbow trout to feed. The Old Dairy Café and BBQ marquee will also cater for peckish humans. Tel: 01223 860374; www.themiltonmaizemaze.co.uk

12

Lode

Get a Lode of This

Stepping out from Lode

Snowdrops are famous round this way – snow joke! But if you are not here in February, you can still see a working watermill, rocket-like trees, a disused railway and, the pièce de résistance, a great big prehistoric toilet where fossilized dinosaur dung was found. Who could resist finding out more?

Lode

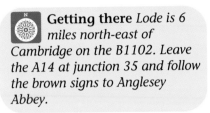 **Getting there** *Lode is 6 miles north-east of Cambridge on the B1102. Leave the A14 at junction 35 and follow the brown signs to Anglesey Abbey.*

Length of walk 4 miles.
Time to allow 2½ hours.
Terrain A mostly flat mix of wooded river banks and lush farm tracks. Beware the unfenced water.
Start/Parking The National Trust car park for Anglesey Abbey.

(GR: TL 534622).
Map OS Explorer 226
Refreshments There is a good National Trust restaurant in the Abbey grounds for a full-on hearty lunch or quick cuppa and cake. Alternatively, drive to the Wheatsheaf in nearby Stow-cum-Quy, a dining pub with a daily carvery and home-cooked grub including half-sized portions for kids. Tel: 01223 812196; www.wheatsheafstowcumquy.co.uk

❶ Walk away from the road,

The Walk

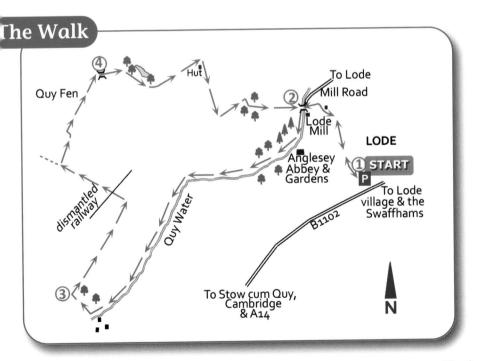

parallel to the hedge bordering the Abbey gardens on your left, to the car park corner. Continue along this path, through a field, a kissing gate, a hedge-lined alley and then out into an open meadow. Veer diagonally left, skirting round the far side of the tennis court to a path which brings you alongside allotments on your right. Now turn left to walk with houses and gardens to your right.

❷ Emerge at Lode Mill on your left. Cross the footbridge, turning immediately left along the water's edge. Continue past the tall rocket-ship poplars on your right. Everybody count down: 10, 9, 8... BLAST OFF! After the river bends right, see who spots the huge bell opposite, and just look at the lily pads on the river! Keep along the meandering water's edge for about a mile, leaving the woodland and heading into open ground. Eventually you'll spot some corrugated stabling on the other bank. Go through a metal kissing gate, then scramble carefully down the diagonal path right. Head sharp right away from the river towards the field corner, hunting out acorns underfoot. You could play 'Squirrel': hide or bury your acorns, spin around until you're dizzy, then come back and see if you can find them.

❸ Go through the kissing gate and turn right along a grassy track sandwiched between fields. Follow the path to the left, then proceed straight over the crossroads (the former Cambridge to Mildenhall railway line) and

◆ Fun Things to See and Do ◆

Do an **A-Z welly wander.** Try to find something on your walk starting with every letter of the alphabet. Write it all down, or test your memory at the end!

Or try a **mini-beast safari,** looking under stones and fallen leaves to see what's lurking. If you're game, you could create your own mini-beasts with your bodies. Join forces to make a 6-legged ladybird, or even a spider. If there are lots of you, split into teams and race!

follow the track until you reach a fork. Turn right between fields and continue to another kissing gate onto Quy Fen. Turn sharp right, following the signed path towards Lode. Pass through a mid-field gate and upon dipping right, through another kissing gate onto a footbridge.

4 Turn 11 o'clock left and head towards a copse where you turn right, the trees and water now on your left. At the end, turn left towards an avenue of trees, then continue until you pass a concrete pre-fab. Turn right, following the track behind the building, and then on towards a T-junction. Here turn left towards approaching woodland. Follow the signposted path into the wood on your right then after about 100 yards, the path forks and you turn left. Continue along the path which emerges onto a field edge and soon go back over the footbridge to Lode Mill. Now retrace your earlier footsteps, to the abbey car park.

Background Notes ◆

Anglesey Priory, built in 1236, once stood on an island. Today Anglesey Abbey can be visited courtesy of the National Trust. Do look out for the dressing up box. Tel: 01223 810080.

Quy Fen is what remains of common land stretching between Horningsea, Quy and Fen Ditton villages. It is now a Site of Special Scientific Interest because of its rare fen plants and the dragonflies and damselflies which breed in the water-filled pits left from coprolite excavation in the 19th century. Coprolite – the polite word for fossilized dinosaur dung – was mined here for use as fertiliser due to its high phosphate content and also for use in the explosives industry.

Nearby Places to Visit
The free Sedgwick Museum of Earth Sciences in Cambridge is the place to find out about coprolite digging and see a wealth of fossils, rocks and minerals. Children's trails are available. Tel: 01223 333456: www.sedgwickmuseum.org

Paxton Pits

Here We Go Round the Blackberry Bush

Is that a heron I can see?

If you come here in early autumn, bring a container with you. With blackberry bushes aplenty, you would kick yourself for missing the chance of a rib-sticking crumble later. Otherwise, keep a look out for warbling nightingales, sun-worshipping cormorants and wild strawberries. You can also see the quarries that played a part in the Second World War, discover an old ferry crossing, or take a moment to imagine a huge woolly mammoth loping by. They really were here once. But don't worry, they're all extinct now. At least we *think* they are …

Paxton Pits

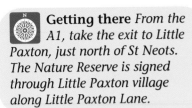

Getting there *From the A1, take the exit to Little Paxton, just north of St Neots. The Nature Reserve is signed through Little Paxton village along Little Paxton Lane.*

Length of walk 2 miles.
Time to allow 1½ hours.
Terrain Mainly surfaced paths. Three kissing gates negotiable by most buggies. The quarry pits are safely fenced, but take care near the open river. Wellies advisable when wet!
Start/Parking The free car park at the reserve entrance. (GR: TL 195629).
Map OS Explorer 225
Refreshments The volunteer-run visitor centre provides hot and cold drinks, crisps, biscuits and ice creams in summer. Otherwise, try the Anchor in Little Paxton, a real-ale pub whose menu boasts home-made pies and a good choice of kids' meals, and there's play equipment including a sunken boat in the garden. Tel. 01480 473199; www.theanchorlittlepaxton.co.uk

1 From the car park, take the board walk over a ditch with the visitor centre to your right. Go through a pair of gateposts; adventurers can scramble up the hillock and join you on the other side. Carefully cross the road and go through the kissing gate into the wide path beyond, with Heronry Lake to your left. Grab some fronds from the willow trees and give yourself a new hair-do! Now walk straight on into

◆ Fun Things to See and Do ◆

Junior palaeontologists will be amazed to hear that woolly mammoths once trod here. Imagine the surprise of the quarry workers when they came upon a huge jawbone complete with a pair of brick-like teeth. They also found a tusk, a tibia and an enormous rib bone, all from a real mammoth. Why not take turns **imagining your very own extinct prehistoric creature**? Think how they walked, what sounds they made, what they ate and perhaps how they smelt! Don't forget to drop into the visitor centre to see the actual bones that were found.

The Walk

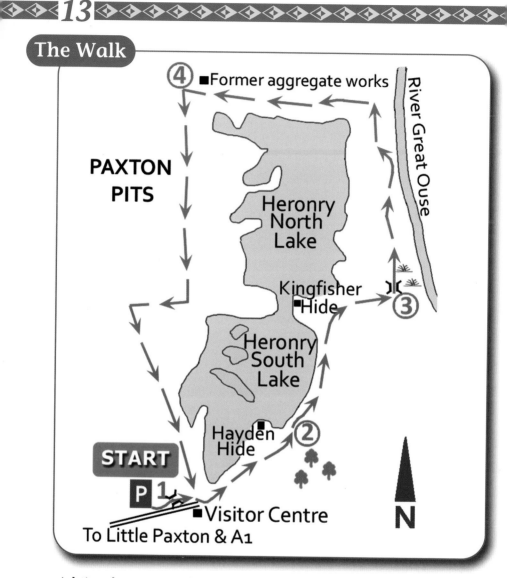

④ ■Former aggregate works

River Great Ouse

PAXTON PITS

Heronry North Lake

Kingfisher ■Hide

③

Heronry South Lake

Hayden ■Hide ②

START

P 1

■Visitor Centre

To Little Paxton & A1

N

nightingale territory. If you're here in spring, you might hear one in the scrubland. Every year the birds fly back from Africa to nest amongst these hawthorn and dog rose bushes. What an incredible journey they make. Just imagine what they're singing about!

Scrambling up the hillock near the car park

❷ Why not step into Hayden Hide left, but do be quiet if there are birdwatchers inside. Who can spot the island, a cormorant stretching its wings in the sun, and perhaps a heron? When leaving, look in the sandy verges for the small white flowers in May or the tiny fruits in July and August of the wild strawberry plant. Continue as the path curves to a fork. You can visit another hide by turning left here along a narrow path to Kingfisher Hide (not suitable for buggies). This secret hideaway, with 180° lake views, is like a castle turret among the oak tree branches. Rejoin the path, continuing past Peter's Field until you reach a public footpath sign.

❸ Follow the sign sharp left across a small brook to join the Ouse Valley Way. It can be wet here (perhaps better named the Ooze Valley Way?) but the moist-loving yellow flag iris loves it. On your right, see who can spot the remains of an old rowing boat. During the 18th century, people crossed by ferry here to get to and fro between Great and Little Paxton. Follow the path alongside the river, then left into a thicket and on through another kissing gate. The towering ivy-clad trees here teem with wildlife – who's feeling itchy at the thought? Take the path 90° to your left and join

Kiddiwalks in Cambridgeshire

the trail running alongside the fenced quarry pits. To detract from the stern but necessary safety warnings, see how many nesting boxes you can spot among the trees to your left.

4 Walk past the Little Paxton gravel works – temporarily closed at the time of writing but still with machinery and huge piles of gravel to look at. Walk over the now-quiet road to a grassy track,

turning 90° left and onwards until crossing the tarmac bridge. Turn immediately right into a wooded path, at the end of which turn sharp left just ahead of a kissing gate and walk on past Rory's Wood. The path here is soft. Who can spot animal tracks in the mud – muntjac deer or a fox perhaps? Emerge onto the road and head towards the gate which brings you back to the start with the car park on your right.

◆ Background Notes ◆

This area was used for thousands of years as farmland until a little under a century ago when the aggregates industry moved in. The first of the pits was dug in the 1930s when dredging of sand and gravel began. Some of the gravel was used for the vast number of wartime runways that were in Cambridgeshire during the Second World War.

The holes that remained after dredging were left to fill with water. Nowadays around 70 species of birds regularly breed here with more coming to overwinter. In total, 234 species have been recorded at Paxton Pits, but the VIP birds are the nightingales. There are also wonderful flowers including dove's foot cranesbill, ox eye daisy, ragged robin and viper's bugloss. Do pop into the **Children's Corner** at the visitor centre where you can find activity sheets, or friendly rangers who can tell you more.

Nearby Places to Visit

You can learn lots more about the Second World War airfields at the **Imperial War Museum** in Duxford. Tel, 01223 835000; www.duxford.iwm.org.uk

14

Woodditton

Devilishly Good Fun

The lush countryside around Woodditton

Y ou are unlikely to find four and twenty blackbirds in a pie here, but three of them will watch you go, and count you back in at the end. In between, you can pick out a giant's Christmas tree, swing on a tree rope if you dare, and discover the fascinating tale of a devilish tail.

Kiddiwalks in Cambridgeshire

14

Getting there
Woodditton is on Cambridgeshire's eastern border. Take the A1303 from Cambridge into Newmarket, turning right onto the B1061 to Dullingham. After 300 yards bear left following the signs to Woodditton. Turn left at the crossroads, parking outside the Three Blackbirds on Ditton Green.

Length of walk 2 miles.
Time to allow 1–1½ hours.
Terrain An easy walk, through woods and fields, a bridleway and a quiet lane.
Start/Parking The Three Blackbirds pub; park on the roadside nearby. (GR: TL 659581)
Map OS Explorer 210
Refreshments The Three Blackbirds, dated 1642, is the perfect country pub.
Tel: 01638 731100; www.thethreeblackbirdswoodditton.co.uk

1 Facing away from the pub, turn right to walk along the pavement admiring the adjacent pebbledash cottages and 'chicken paddock' to your left. Count the chickens and give them each a name. As Ditton Green changes to Stetchworth Road, follow it as it bends right then left. Don't go down the track next to the water tower but continue along the

♦ Fun Things to See and Do ♦

Being close to Newmarket, why not **take an imaginary horse for a ride**? Mount with extravagance, clip clop around and tether up when you dismount for water and oats. You might be a mounted musketeer with a stick sword, or perhaps a show-jumper cresting fallen branch obstacles!

Or **go on a texture hunt** and see how many different textures you find. There might be tickly grasses, flaky bark, glossy chestnuts, prickly pine cones, squelchy mud, waxy leaves or lacy cow parsley and more. Go on, wiggle your fingers and get touching. Have fun, but do remember to wash your hands before lunch!

The Walk

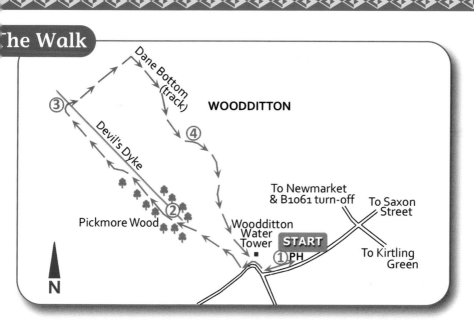

Dane Bottom (track)

WOODDITTON

③

④

Devil's Dyke

Pickmore Wood

②

To Newmarket & B1061 turn-off

To Saxon Street

Woodditton Water Tower

START

① PH

To Kirtling Green

N

roadside grass verge. After number 14 take the public footpath on the right towards Reach 7½ miles, past gardens, a low bench, and across an arable field. At the other side you enter Pickmore Wood. Do you suppose there are elves living inside? What do you think they pick more of?

❷ Follow the woodland path as it meanders right and gently downhill. On your right is the Devil's Dyke. Older children can zoom down the banks and swing on the rope (Tarzan holler obligatory!). Otherwise, try spotting which trees are deciduous or coniferous, or which would make the best giant's

Christmas tree! Ignore the fingerpost pointing left but continue straight over a dip to emerge at the corner of the wood under a mature oak. Turn right to walk alongside the woodland boundary. Go through a gap in the hedgerow and continue, with fields and the village of Stetchworth on your distant left.

❸ When you get to a T-junction, turn right and scramble up the bank of Devil's Dyke, crossing the Stour Valley Way at the top. Drop back down the slope towards the open fields. This is part of the ancient Icknield Way long-distance path. Walk straight on between the fields with sweeping views to your left, then downhill towards some raised steps which you ascend. Turn right onto the track known as Dane Bottom. Continue until the path forks, taking the right option (effectively straight on) onto a narrower grassy path. Go through the five-bar gate, admiring the views behind as you close it. Do mind the electric fence.

④ When the path forks, dip to the left following the blue bridleway arrow. The path gently curves to the right around an old barn, past some stables and between paddocks. Turn left as the grassy path joins a hard track opposite a bungalow. Walk out through the pedestrian access to the side of a five-bar gate. The lane, with lush banks to each side, climbs gently uphill and left. At the top you'll notice the water tower again on your left. Emerge onto the corner of the road and retrace your steps to your car.

◆ Background Notes ◆

The name Woodditton is thought to originate from 'the wood at the end of the ditch'. The ditch in question is the **Devil's Dyke**, one of the country's largest and best surviving examples of an Anglo-Saxon earthwork. In places it is 30m wide and 18m high, charting a near perfect straight line for 7½ miles. Current thinking is that the dyke was originally dug around the 6th century AD as a defensive barrier marking tribal boundaries. However, in the post-medieval period people thought that a landform such as this could only have been made supernaturally – hence the devilish name. A local story tells how the Devil turned up without invitation to a nearby wedding. The angry guests chased him off, but in turn the Devil was so furious that as he ran he slashed out the groove of the dyke with his fiery tail!

Nearby Places to Visit

Newmarket, just over the border in Suffolk, is horseracing central. Why not visit the **National Horseracing Museum** with a Fun Tour and dressing-up opportunities for the children? Tel. 01638 667333; www.nhrm.co.uk Or see the horses themselves in action at **Newmarket Racecourses**. Tel: 0844 579 3010; www.newmarketracecourses.co.uk

15

Grantchester Meadows

Meadow Madness

Admiring the swans and cygnets on the River Cam

Come and explore the Grantchester Grind, a path that many a Cambridge student has trodden before you – though we think it sounds like the name of a silly dance, perhaps one you can make up as you wander along! There is also spire-spotting and pond-dipping to be done (take nets!) or find out about a very famous clock. If that's not enough, then settle down awhile to watch the punters go by. Some are good at it, some are less so. If you're lucky (shhh) you might see someone take an unplanned dip in the river. Splash!

Kiddiwalks in Cambridgeshire

Getting there
Grantchester lies 2 miles south-west of Cambridge. Leave the M11 at junction 12 from which Grantchester is signposted. Turn right at the T-junction opposite the Rupert Brooke pub.

Length of walk 2¼ miles.
Time to allow 1½ hours.
Terrain An easy 'there and back' walk, the first half being flat tarmac, ideal for buggies. The return loop by the river can be boggy, so bring wellies in wetter periods. (Buggies can always repeat the higher path.)
Start/Parking At or near the Green Man and Red Lion pubs. In peak periods use the signposted charity car park and walk back to the start point. (GR: TL 433556).
Map OS Explorer 209
Refreshments Grantchester

boasts several great pubs including the Red Lion which has a children's menu and garden play equipment. Tel. 01223 840121; www.redlion-grantchester.co.uk. For genteel refreshment, try The Orchard tea garden. Tel. 01223 845788. Otherwise, take a picnic to the meadows.

1 With the Red Lion pub on your left and the Green Man on your right, walk towards a wooden five-bar gate and over the first of many dainty cattle grids – always fun to wobble over. Turn left onto the tarmac track, in fact a cycle path to Cambridge nicknamed the Grantchester Grind. Look to the right for the spires of King's College Chapel and the Catholic church in Cambridge. Walk straight onwards via a series of gateways

◆ Fun Things to See and Do ◆

If you have nets and a bucket, bring them along for **minnow dipping**. Or take inspiration from the dapperly-dressed punting crowd and **make a badge or hair accessory**. Look out for eye-catching fallen natural objects, unusually-shaped, tinted or textured.
Gather them together with string from the backpack and wear in your hair or on a coat button – the most creative wins!

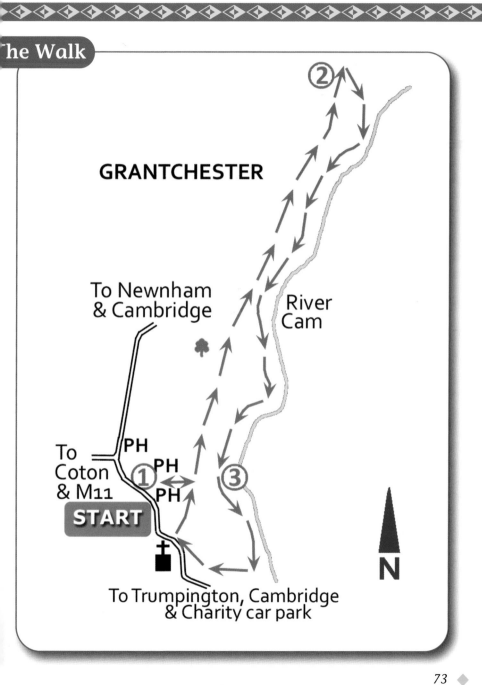

GRANTCHESTER

To Newnham
& Cambridge

River
Cam

To
Coton
& M11

PH

PH

PH

① ② ③

START

To Trumpington, Cambridge
& Charity car park

N

and mini cattle grids with the River Cam meandering off over the meadows to your right. Avoid the temptation to walk closer to it – your return leg takes you back along the river bank. There should be rich blackberry pickings in the hedges here in season, as well as – beware – the odd rich cow pat under your feet!

2 Look for the public footpath sign pointing you right, just ahead of an oak tree and a metal gate into a narrower alley. Turn sharp right off the tarmac track here and over a wooden boardwalk. As you near the river, veer right to walk with the Cam on your left. There may be cattle grazing hereabouts with individually numbered 'earrings'. Continue along the winding river, looking out for dragonflies, swooping birds and perhaps the odd angler. Cross the first of several footbridges, pass three weeping willows, and then go on via a series of bridges and gates along the river's edge, meandering with the bends of the river. Keep looking out for tiddlers in the shallows, moorhens or even people passing by in boats. The brave might like to warn them not to fall in – you never know there might be piranhas in the water!

The route across the meadows

3 Stay on the lower level close to the river bank, looking out for a pair of tall chopped-off tree trunks as the river bears left. Go through the gate beside the trees and veer left, still keeping along the river bank. You may see swans sitting on their nest here in season, or try counting the cygnets! After going through another gate labelled 'no barbecues or fires' turn sharp right. At the top of the field, go through the green gate slightly off-left and emerge onto a gently climbing gravel track. Stop if you wish for drinks on the inviting deckchairs of The Orchard tea garden to your left. Otherwise, at the bend of the road, turn right into Mill Way (effectively straight on) admiring St Andrew and St Mary's church as you go. This is the one with the famous clock though you'll have to detour over to see it. Now take the public footpath signed to your right towards Newnham 1½ miles past the alluringly-named Snug Cottage and Green Man pub. Go over another mini cattle grid, then left where you entered the meadows to retrace your steps to the start.

Background Notes ◆

Should you stop for refreshments in The Orchard, you're following in the footsteps of a group of Cambridge University students who in 1897 persuaded the owner of Orchard House to serve them tea. It was the start of a now long-established tradition for students and tourists to punt along the river to Grantchester and take tea at Orchard House where the poet Rupert Brooke once lodged. There is a free onsite Rupert Brooke museum where you can learn more about him and his famous poems including the one about the church clock which stood at ten to three.

Nearby Places to Visit

Byron's Pool, just on Grantchester's outskirts, is named after Lord Byron (1788–1824) who is said to have swum here whilst studying at Trinity College. The tranquil woodland area is now a nature reserve – look out for frogspawn in the smaller ponds in spring, or listen for the steady drum of a woodpecker.

If the thought of Byron splashing makes you yearn for a swim, **Parkside Pool** in Cambridge has three pools, including a play area complete with slides and bubble jets. Tel 01223 446100. Or if hot, there's the hugely popular **Lammas Land Paddling Pool** and playground in nearby Newnham, Cambridge.

16

The Gransdens
A Grand Day Out!

Chickens galore!

Hundreds of fluffy chickens, some magnificent horses and a field of winsome alpacas make this a walk for would-be farmers. For those less animal-inclined, however, there's plenty more, including a fighter plane stained-glass window, a magical bluebell wood in spring, blackberries in autumn and a trot past a sewage farm which *could* make for rich conversation, but will *definitely* make for speedier walking!

The Gransdens

Getting there *The Gransdens lie off the A428 between the A1 and Cambridge. Take the B1040 at Eltisley, turning left after 2 miles onto the B1046. Pass through Great Gransden and then at Little Gransden take the first right (where the main road turns 90° left) into Church Street.*

Length of walk 4 miles.
Time to allow At least 2½ hours.
Terrain Muddy in places so bring the wellies if wet. Overall, mixed terrain with wooded paths, country tracks and a village meander.
Start/Parking Church Street opposite Little Gransden church. (GR: TL 270552).
Map OS Explorer 208

Refreshments There are two pubs in the Gransdens for crisps, drinks and loo stops but they don't do daytime meals. You could try Great Gransden Post Office Stores on Fox Street for basic provisions or bring a picnic to enjoy on Brownes' Piece.

1 Head slightly uphill along Church Street, past pretty cottages including a pheasant-topped thatch. Ignore the footpath sign left but continue past a field of alpacas on your right and a duck pond des-res at Willow Tree House. Ignore also the bridleway right, continuing straight on as the lane narrows. There are rich blackberry pickings here in autumn. After about ½ mile, the path turns sharp right. Proceed along it with a ditch and open

◆ Fun Things to See and Do ◆

Walking through a chicken farm, you're bound to find feathers on the floor. Look out for light fluffy ones, then have **a keepy-uppy competition**, wafting and blowing to see who can keep theirs in the air the longest without touching.

Hunt for tree faces in the wood. Look closely and knobbly tree trunks can magically reveal a mossy nose and winking eyes. Use your hands to make flappy ears, or a stick to make an impish smile!

The Walk

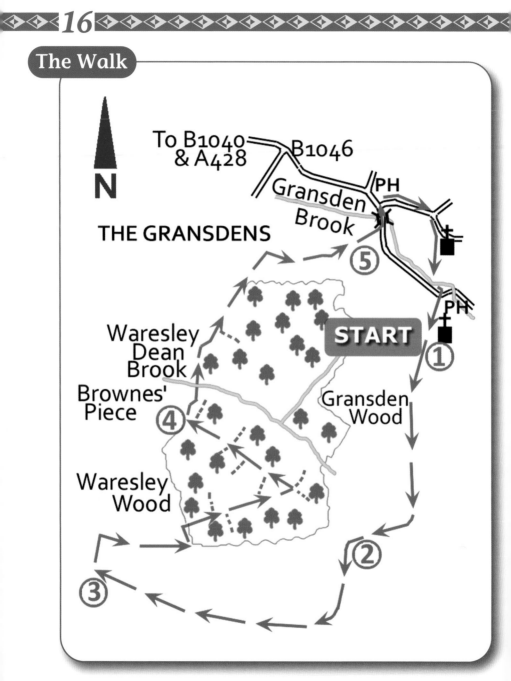

To B1040 & A428

B1046

Gransden Brook

PH

THE GRANSDENS

⑤

START

①

Waresley Dean Brook

Gransden Wood

Brownes' Piece

④

Waresley Wood

②

③

N

field to your left and a hedgerow to your right.

2 After about ⅓ mile, turn 90° left to walk alongside a patchy hedgerow and grassy bank with cowslips and bluebells in season. Upon reaching a T-junction, turn right towards a red and white striped gas post. Cross a ditch and continue forwards. Who can spot the church spire? Carry on as the track bears right, past a black wooden fence, with trees and hawthorn hedges to the right. At the black five-bar gate, pass through the pedestrian access into an avenue of mature hedges among horses and chickens galore!

Alpacas lazing in the sunshine

benches. Look out for moss-covered tree stumps, home to tiny fairies perhaps? Ignore the smaller paths off, but continue straight towards the distant five-bar gate, going through the adjacent kissing gate.

3 Just before the farmyard, turn right along the signed footpath with the farmhouse to your left. Turn right at the corner around the perimeter of the field – careful near the electric fences. The path dog-legs past an oak tree then continues to the corner of the wood where you turn sharp left. The wood, now on your right, is entered by a concealed gate dedicated to Bruno's owner (who or what was Bruno do you think?). In spring, the wood is filled with magical glades of deepest bluebells. Turn left at the crossroads at the second of two

4 If you need a rest or a picnic stop, head for Brownes' Piece through the next gate. Otherwise, turn directly right with the metal fence on your left, the wood on your right. At this point you'll notice the sewage farm on your left. The aroma can be quite arresting but it's a ripe opportunity for discussing what happens after you flush and, anyway, which child doesn't enjoy a bit of toilet talk? Follow this winding path upwards. Emerge onto an open field, then dip back into the trees briefly before coming back to the field edge. Continue, descending gradually, then as the hedgerow bends round slip through the gap in the trees on your right. Turn left here to follow the path down and around the meadow. Ignore the first stile left, continuing to the second stile ahead which takes you onto a track past a thatched cottage.

5 Emerge onto the corner of the road next to Jankins Cottage. Cross over onto the grass verge and turn left. Head carefully over the bridge and turn right onto Cow Tree Street. You'll need to cross at number 14 to the footpath opposite and then back again after Old Tailor's House.

Continue forward past the mini roundabout into Church Street. Turn right into the churchyard, looking inside to admire the window commemorating 405 RCAF Pathfinder Squadron who were based at Gransden Lodge airfield during the Second World War. Continue descending the churchyard path and over another footbridge. Take the right path towards a kissing gate, heading for Little Gransden church tower. Continue towards a wooden kissing gate, over another bridge and up to the road. Turn left along the pavement, crossing carefully at the corner, back into Church Street and to your car.

◆ Background Notes ◆

Waresley and Gransden Woods, owned by the Cambridgeshire Wildlife Trust, are adjacent ancient oak and ash woods separated by a small stream. Beautiful in spring with bluebells, oxslips and violets aplenty, there is also an abundance of wild flowers and insects to be found in the rides and glades in summer. These include the speckled wood butterfly, one of the 500 species of moth and butterfly that have been recorded here. For more information visit www.waresleywood.co.uk

Nearby Places to Visit
The annual **Little Gransden Families Day Out** Air & Vintage Vehicle Show held each August; www.littlegransdenshow.co.uk

Wandlebury Country Park

Cross the Sleeping Giants If You Dare!

Highland cattle, seen grazing on the walk

The Gog Magog Hills just outside Cambridge disprove the theory that the county is flat. On top is Wandlebury Country Park where you'll find the remains of an ancient hill fort, an underground ice house, and the grave of an Arabian stallion with history – the great, great.... grandfather of many of today's racehorses. What's more, there's a bat colony, the crash site of a Second World War Wellington bomber, and under the hills, they say, lie the slumbering giants Gog and Magog. Do be careful not to step on a hairy nostril as you go!

Kiddiwalks in Cambridgeshire

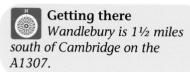

Getting there
Wandlebury is 1½ miles south of Cambridge on the A1307.

Length of walk 1¾ miles.
Time to allow At least 1 hour.
Terrain All off-road, clearly marked woodchip paths. Suitable for robust buggies.
Start/Parking The Wandlebury Country Park car park; fee payable. (GR: TL 492532).
Map OS Explorer 209
Refreshments Wandlebury is

perfect for picnics. There is a pre-bookable BBQ (call the Head Ranger on 07833 598155) and on summer weekends the Icycle Tricycle serves traditional ice-cream, sorbets and cold drinks from a renovated 1920s trike. Otherwise, a short car journey will take you to the excellent Gog Magog Hills Farm Shop and Café. Tel. 01223 248352; www.gogmagoghills.com

❶ Head uphill away from the road, past the noticeboard, and on through a metal gateway.

The Walk

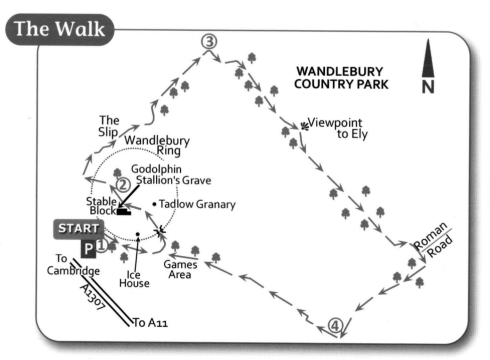

Follow the main tarmac path ahead, with a line of trees to your right and pond-dipping platforms to your left. Bear left over the brick bridge that traverses the sunken Wandlebury Ring. Anyone with excess energy can run around it later! Explorers could investigate the brick tower, hard left, with views of an underground tunnel to the ice house, nowadays a home to bats. There's also Tadlow Granary, a sun dial, and the former stables and cupola clock under which lies the Godolphin Arabian's grave. See who finds it first. What age did the stallion live to?

2 With your back to the stable block, head left to the doorway in the long garden wall marked post 1. Go through Scarisbrick Gate into the old orchard, over a ditch crossroads and onto the outer path at post 2. In early spring, this is awash with snowdrops and aconites. To the left is where the Wellington bomber crashed in 1941. A piece of the tailfin remained stuck in a tree until it was chopped down in 1991 – the wreckage is on display at the Tower Museum in Bassingbourn (Herts). Turn right and when you get to post 3, turn left. After a dog-leg, enter an avenue of trees. This path, known as the Slip, was the training ground for the Earl of Godolphin's racehorses. Today you might see rather more sedate Highland cattle grazing here instead.

3 Bear right at post 4 and see who first finds 5, then 6. Turn left at this point into a woodland path. The Gog Magog golf course is on your left – there are birdies of both sorts on this walk! On clear days you can see Ely Cathedral 17½ miles away. At

◆ Fun Things to See and Do ◆

Take a cricket set, a frisbee or ball. Or why not **stage a horse race** to honour the Godolphin Stallion? Look for large sticks along the walk and use coats, jumpers and bags to make fences on your own Godolphin Grand National course. Race in pairs, or time contestants over the obstacles. Extra points for loud 'giddy ups' to gee up your trusty steeds.

post 7, turn right and then left at number 8. At post 10 (you've skipped 9!) note the encircled 'bonsai' beech tree which, due to a genetic fault, remained exceptionally small. How tall are you next to it? The path now heads downhill past post 11 where you turn left, and then skirts right around a private house. Ignore the Roman road to the left but turn right shortly afterwards onto another woodland path. Continue until you reach a 90° right turn.

4 Walk straight on until you curve left around a games area. This was formerly a bowling green and later the servants' cricket pitch. It is an ideal place to stop for a picnic or to organise your own cricket match or clamber on the fallen tree. When done, proceed past the brick bridge you crossed earlier, now on your right, and retrace your steps to the start.

◆ Background Notes ◆

Amongst Wandlebury Country Park's treasures are the remains of an **Iron Age hill fort** from the 5th century BC. The clearest visible evidence of this Scheduled Ancient Monument is the circular ring ditch, and it is thought that the remains of the Iron Age fort lie undisturbed beneath the old terraced lawns. Periodically, pieces of pottery or flints are found in mole hills here.

Under the cupola clock archway to the stables is a tablet commemorating the great **Godolphin Arabian** whose romantic tale you can read in Marguerite Henry's classic *King of the Wind*. The real Godolphin (c1724–1754), was brought to Gogmagog Hall in the early 18th century. Also known as the Godolphin Barb, he was one of three Arabian stallions that founded the modern Thoroughbred racing bloodstock.

During weekends and school holidays, the **Cambridge Past, Present and Future Society** runs a great programme of events for children suh as 'Watery Wonders' for supervised pond-dipping, a 'Nature Safari' for young nature detectives, and the chance to 'Travel Back Through Time' which involves getting very messy making 'wattle and daub' panels! Tel: 01223 243830 or www.cambridgeppf.org for bookings.

18

Wimpole Estate
A Bit of Park Life

Striding out from Wimpole Hall

W ho knows if a nun's head-covering is a wimple or a wimpole? Though this walk has nothing to do with nuns, with open spaces all around, you could happily do *The Hills Are Alive* renditions in the style of Julie Andrews here. If that's not your thing, enjoy instead the simpler pleasures of walking amongst grazing livestock and venerable old trees with a folly, a Chinese bridge and a waterfowl-filled lake thrown in for luck. Just try not to throw your *Favourite Things*-warbling sister in too, won't you?

Kiddiwalks in Cambridgeshire

Getting there *Start at Arrington on the A1198, the old Ermine Street, 17½ miles south of Huntingdon, or 8½ miles south-west of Cambridge off the A603.*

Length of walk 4 miles.
Time to allow 2½ hours.
Terrain All off-road, a stile and a couple of steep banks, mixing woodland trails and open parkland.
Start/Parking Church Lane opposite the Hardwicke Arms. (GR: TL 328502).
Map OS Explorer 209
Refreshments Bring a picnic or try one of the National Trust eateries such as the Stable Kitchen for light refreshments and ice creams. If only a pub will do, the Hardwicke Arms Hotel serves cosy indoor meals, but for

a family-welcome, beer garden and play equipment, try the Queen Adelaide Inn, just west of Arrington in Croydon. Tel. 01223 208278; www.queen-adelaide.co.uk

1 Cross the A1198, heading left towards the imposing Wimpole Estate gates. Enter the park through the black gate then walk the gently curving track towards Wimpole Hall. After a cattle grid and gate, turn immediately left alongside a wire fence with the hall on your right. You might want a rest at the top – stop and make hand shadows if it's sunny. Now head towards the trees, veering right to walk parallel with them. You'll pass West Avenue, sweeping down to the house on your right, but your scouts should look for the kissing gate ahead which takes you onto Lime

◆ Fun Things to See and Do ◆

The information boards show pictures of a rusty-red click beetle, brown-lipped snail, barbastelle bat and merveille du jour moth. It would be great to see, or even hear, some of them. Find a quiet place to stop and listen. Shut your eyes **and try counting ten different sounds**, either natural or perhaps the noise of an aeroplane. Share what you heard. What do you think the trees are whispering?

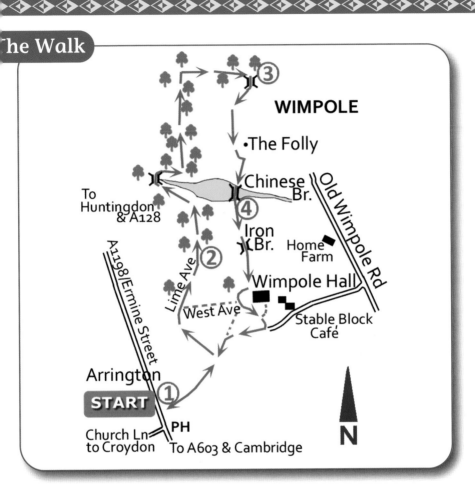

Avenue (c1800). Find the information sign up ahead. Which drink is made from dried lime-tree flowers?

2 Now climb over the metal stile beside the five-bar gate into the Woodland Belt. Follow the path downhill with glimpses of a lake on your right. At the foot of the hill, cross a ditch before the trail bends left. Continue until you reach the edge of the wood when the path crosses water and turns back on the other side. The path soon swings 90° left and then climbs. At the T-junction, turn right and slightly downhill. Ignore the farm track right, but proceed towards a dip. Near the

Kiddiwalks in Cambridgeshire

bottom, before the path heads up again, turn right through a brambly footpath towards a wooden footbridge.

❸ Emerge onto the corner of a rolling arable field. Walk straight ahead along the grassy path following the field edge. Go through the end gate then veer 45° left up the grassy bank towards the folly. Walk around the perimeter fence until you get to the front. Although you can't get to the folly, why not count the windows and arrow crosses? Now turn right towards the lake, heading for a lone tree behind which lies the Grade II listed Chinese Bridge. Just look at the

magnificent finial balls – marbles for giants perhaps?

❹ Now head towards the hall rooftops, bearing slightly left and over the Iron Bridge. Continue towards the house, veering right to go anti-clockwise around the railings. Go through another kissing gate, emerging to sweeping views of the ha-ha and stone cherubs on your left. Skirt the gardens next to the railings on the left, through another gate, and then cut to the gravelled drive before the house. The stable block with a café and loos is a short walk ahead. Otherwise turn right at the end of the drive, back along the lane to Arrington.

◆ Background Notes ◆

Wimpole Hall was built in 1643 for the 3rd Earl of Hardwicke and eventually developed into the largest country house in Cambridgeshire. The last private owner was Mrs Elsie Bambridge, daughter of Rudyard Kipling. Today the house is owned by the National Trust so you can explore its treasures, which include an enormous plunge bath, large enough for two cricket teams!

Nearby Places to Visit
Wimpole Home Farm runs hands-on farm activities such as grooming the donkeys, feeding the goats and animal bath-time. There's an adventure playground, with a Kidbine Harvester and pedal tractors in front of the farm café. Tel. 01223 206000; www.nationaltrust.org.uk/main/w-wimpole-estate

19

Thriplow

Take a Trip to Thriplow

Along the way

Aviation experts will be over the moon (or over a cloud perhaps) if they walk this route on a display day. During air-shows at Duxford, you get the next best thing to a ringside view! If it's not a flying day then don't despair. With a pillbox which contains no pills, a blacksmith that is white, and a green man who is actually blue, young Sherlocks can come here and solve a mystery or two!

Kiddiwalks in Cambridgeshire

Getting there *Leave the M11 at junction 10 and head towards Royston on the A505. After 1½ miles turn right towards Thriplow, and left at the T-junction in the village to the Green Man pub.*

Length of walk 3 miles.
Time to allow 1½ hours.
Terrain A mixed bag of meadow trails, farm tracks and concrete bridleways (good for scooters!). A couple of stretches along quiet roadways.
Start/Parking Fowlmere Road anywhere near the Green Man pub. (GR: TL 436466).
Map OS Explorer 209
Refreshments The Green Man is happy to accommodate families with half-size portions of anything on the menu. Outside there's a giant Jenga and Connect 4, and inside you'll find a toy box with train, cars, a tea set and books. Tel. 01763 208855; www.greenmanthriplow.co.uk

1 Start outside the Green Man pub which, confusingly, is blue. Turn into Lower Street and proceed for 200 yards. Just before the road curves right, turn left before Yew Tree Cottage. See who spots the public footpath sign hidden in the ivy. Head into the alleyway to the right of the house, continuing until you reach the road. Turn left, cross safely and go along the footpath signed right after 50 yards. Walk down the tarmac lane which changes to

♦ Fun Things to See and Do ♦

Why not pop over to the white-washed **Thriplow Smithy**? See when it was presented to the village by Robert J. Younger Esquire. Though it is out of use at present, just imagine it surrounded by snorting horses with a steaming anvil at the centre.

Play **Walkie Word Association**. One player says a word inspired by something on the walk, eg wellies. The next person thinks of something connected, eg 'mud' and so on. After a few turns, see if you can jog backwards and remember all the words in reverse order.

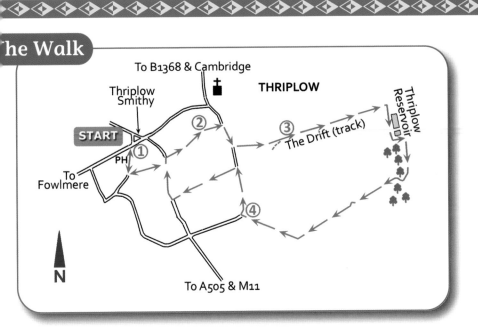

a track. Go through over-arching trees and past chicken sheds, clucking hellos to the hens, until you reach a kissing gate.

2 Emerge into a meadow, following the track under low branches, veering right, after a dead tree trunk, towards a row of houses. Go through a second kissing gate, cross to the footpath opposite and turn right. Who can spot the well on the left? Take care of traffic here. In 200 yards, after the Narnia lamppost and before the thatched house, take the bridleway left. Head slightly uphill and out into open fields – beware the mud here if it has been wet. Look over your

shoulder (or upside down between your legs!) at the church spire and stop for some Second World War history when you find the old airfield-defending pillbox. Who's brave and fancies a poke around inside?

3 Continue as your path joins another farm track at a birdlife board – how many birds are pictured? After ambling downhill, cross a ditch and turn 90° right signposted ½ mile to Heathfield taking you past Thriplow reservoir on your left (take care, it is unfenced). Just beyond the reservoir, the path turns left and then right, through an avenue of trees. It then loops around a clump of trees and meets a concrete roadway where you turn right, signposted to Thriplow ¾ mile. Walk with the hedge to your left, past a pond and bench, until you reach some industrial buildings. At the main entrance to the premises, turn, at 2 o'clock, along the avenue of new trees.

4 After the yellow gates at the end, turn right along the grass verge. Continue along the lane passing an ivy-clad tree stump. We reckon it's like a lying-down horse, what do you think? Continue until you reach a public footpath on the left after Manor Farm. Follow it alongside the tall hedge, admiring the tiny old window-panes on the left. After the tennis court, take the path to the left between the fences. Go through the trees to a kissing gate and into a meadow. Walk alongside Thriplow Manor garden on your right, with snowdrops and aconites, then daffodils, in season. Go through the kissing gate on the far side and then turn right. Once again, beware of traffic. Just before number 14 turn left along the path you came down earlier, and retrace your steps to the car.

◆ Background Notes ◆

Thriplow, though seemingly sleepy, is host each year to up to 10,000 visitors for its annual **Daffodil Weekend**. The event began in 1969, originally to raise funds for repairs to St George's church, but continues today collecting money for numerous charities. There is plenty besides the flowers, including heavy-horse dray rides, magic shows and maypole dancing. Tel: 01359 233200; www.thriplow.org.uk

Nearby Places to Visit

Next door is the **Duxford Imperial War Museum** which is based on a former First and Second World War airfield. With frequent air shows and family activities, a Concorde to walk through and plenty of hands-on exhibits, this is a must for aviation fans. Tel. 01223 835000; www.duxford.iwm.org.uk

20

Linton

Reach for the Sky!

Come on, it's not deep!

Prepare for fresh air at one of the highest points in East Anglia. A steep climb, yes, but worth it to view a distant Second World War aircraft hangar, pass a cloud-grazing water tower and even find an astronaut at the top! Luckily you won't need oxygen masks yourselves, but you could bring a ball for a great game, some crusts for the ducks, and your wellies for some serious splashing in one of the *two* fords!

Kiddiwalks in Cambridgeshire

Getting there *Linton lies to the south-east of Cambridge on the A1307 to Haverhill. The High Street runs directly off the A1307.*

Length of walk 3 miles.
Time to allow 1½ hours.
Terrain Lots of village walking, a steep climb and a riverbank path. Bring wellies for splashing!
Start/Parking Patrons can park at the Dog and Duck, or overshoot to Coles Lane car park, 2nd left after the pub, backtracking on foot to start the walk. (GR: TL 560468).
Map OS Explorer 209
Refreshments The Dog and Duck is an intriguing mix of traditional country boozer and authentic Italian eatery. Smaller portions of good Italian main meals are available for the children. Tel. 01223 891257; www.doganducklinton.co.uk

1 From the pub, turn right into Meadow Lane, part of the Icknield Way. Go through the white gate into a recreation and cricket ground. Continue straight then turn sharp right, following the path past the cricket pavilion. Cross the footbridge over the River Granta, take the right fork (effectively straight on) and continue to the road. Cross over, skirt around the wire fence left, then right onto the pathway between a brick wall and hedge. Walk through the bungalow estate to a T-junction, turning right out of Crabtree Croft towards the bridleway to Rivey Hill,

◆ Fun Things to See and Do ◆

Camping Close was on village maps in the 1600s. People used to play a special ball game here. Why not **play a Stuck in the Mud ball game** of your own – who knows, maybe another family will do the same 400 years from now? Rules of Football Stuck in the Mud: Everyone runs around trying to evade the person with the football, who is 'It'. If you get touched by the football, you must freeze, legs apart, until another player crawls through your legs to free you. When everyone is 'out', exhausted, or a time limit is up, swap over so that everyone has a turn being 'It'.

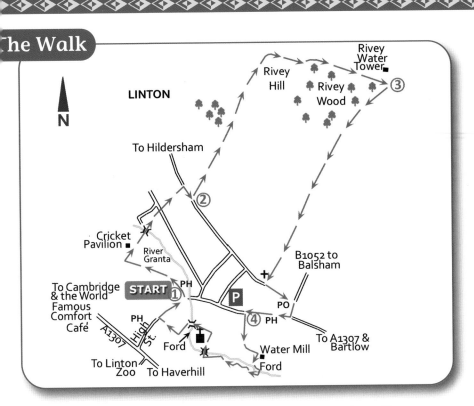

N

LINTON

To Hildersham

Rivey
Hill

Rivey
Wood

Rivey
Water
Tower

③

②

Cricket
Pavilion ■

River
Granta

To Cambridge
& the World
Famous
Comfort
Café

START ①

PH

A1307

High St.

PH

Ford

Ford

To Linton
Zoo

To Haverhill

P

PO

④ PH

Water Mill

B1052 to
Balsham

To A1307 &
Bartlow

50 yards along. (Definitely not Skivey Hill – see how steep it gets!)

❷ Head up the grassy track – here's where it gets steep but there's a welcome bench at the top. Enjoy the patchwork field views and look on the horizon for hangars at the disused Little Walden airfield, former home to USA Air Force bombers during the Second World War. Once rested, turn 90° right (possibly impersonating a fighter plane) along the ridge of Rivey Hill

towards the wood. Walk alongside it towards the red-brick water tower, entering an avenue of trees. On passing the houses, see who spots the astronaut weather vane and gatepost gargoyles (who do you think they look like?). Don't forget to squint to the top of the 92-ft water tower.

❸ At the T-junction, turn right, heading back downhill. It can be wet underfoot here – satisfyingly squelchy but do take care. At the bottom, the path levels out, runs

Kiddiwalks in Cambridgeshire

between houses and emerges next to a cemetery where you turn left. At the T-junction turn right past the post office, then right again onto the High Street. Continue past the Wagon and Horses and Co-op store until you reach Mill Lane where you turn left.

4 Proceed carefully down the lane, turning right before the watermill and under the gangways. Now follow the road around to the first ford and footbridge. (This ford is flooded only after heavy rain so save splashing for the next one.) Turn right along the river bank, ignore the first footbridge and cross the second one into St Mary's churchyard. Right of here is Camping Close, ideal for picnics and ball games. Otherwise continue along the tarmac path, turning left at the crossroads in the churchyard. Leave through the white gateway, crossing to the path to the left of the timber-framed Guildhall, then head to the appropriately-named Duck Bridge. This is the place to get paddling and feed the hungry ducks. When done, proceed along the quiet lane, left then right, and emerge back onto the High Street. Turn right to return to the start.

◆ Background Notes ◆

Linton is renowned for its listed buildings and was one of the first villages designated as a conservation area. A fine example is the former **Guildhall** built c1523, now a beautiful timber-framed private home. Just imagine, it was built when Henry VIII was on the throne!

Next to the church is an area known as **Camping Close** which is now the village green. The name derives from the medieval football game 'camping' which was popular in East Anglia. It was a rather rough version of football played after church on Sundays which is why the fields, like Linton's, are usually adjacent to the church.

Nearby Places to Visit
Why not visit **Linton Zoo**? As well as the animals, picnic spots and a seasonal coffee shop, you'll find children's play areas for all ages including a 'Secret Garden' for under 5s. Tel. 01223 891308.